YOU ALREADY KNEW

D1620475

You Already Knew

Reclamation of your innate childhood
wisdom is not about looking back, it's about bringing forth.

ISBN: 978-0-6454809-0-0 (Print)

ISBN: 978-0-6454809-1-7 (eBook)

The information contained in this book is general in nature and does
not take into account your personal situation. You should consider
whether the information is appropriate to your needs, and where
appropriate, seek professional advice.

Published by Akuna Concepts Books

www.akunaconcepts.com

welcome@akunaconcepts.com

Cover Design by Ellie Schroeder

Photography by Brendan Haack

Printed on demand in Australia

A catalogue record for this
book is available from the
National Library of Australia

YOU ALREADY KNEW

**RECLAMATION OF YOUR
INNATE CHILDHOOD WISDOM
IS NOT ABOUT LOOKING BACK,
IT'S ABOUT BRINGING FORTH.**

Zoe Haack

CONTENTS

Acknowledgement of Country vii

Dedication ix

Introduction 1

Section One - Solid Foundation 13

Chapter One - Human-being. 15

Chapter Two - Values 33

Chapter Three - Beliefs 45

Chapter Four - Attunement 57

Chapter Five - Co-regulated and connected 63

Section Two - Wisdom you were born with 81

Chapter Six - Rituals 83

Chapter Seven - I can do it 91

Chapter Eight - Words matter 105

Chapter Nine - Osmosis 113

Chapter Ten - Play is purposeful.. 129

Section Three - Who your kids need you to be. 139

Chapter Eleven - Present 141

Chapter Twelve - Truthful and Trustworthy 153

Chapter Thirteen - Activists 167

Call to Action 183

Acknowledgements 185

ACKNOWLEDGEMENT OF COUNTRY

My life began on Larrakia land. A stunningly beautiful, wild, and plentiful land. Throughout my life, I have had the immense pleasure of also coming to know the lands of the Gubbi Gubbi, Ngaro and Kalkadoon people. I will, however, always call Larrakia land home. Each place I have been fortunate to call home has shown me the interconnected nature of country.

Aboriginal people have been raising their children with a deep and purposeful connection to country for thousands of years. Their collective knowledge and capacity to share knowledge through the ages solidify for me the importance of raising children with a deep connection to themselves, their kin and country.

I acknowledge our nation's first people as the true and rightful custodians of the land which sustains us. I pay my respects to all indigenous people and make a commitment to deepening my understanding of traditional ways of living on and caring for country.

I invite you to join me in drawing upon our nation's first people's wisdom in your parenting practice. We have much to gain from doing so.

DEDICATION

This book is dedicated to my children Hailey and Wahri.

Hailey, you've shown me what it is to be a Mum. You've been by my side as I've navigated what 'Mother' means, and all it has shifted within me. I gained the courage to become a birth Mother as a result of coming to know you. Bearing witness to your journey is a true gift.

Wahri, you brought me home to me, the me I have always been. Your birth transformed me and opened me up to broader possibilities. Your capacity for love and connection extends beyond the bounds of what I knew to be possible. Joining with you as you navigate the world is a treasure.

Hailey and Wahri, may you remain deeply connected to your innate wisdom and intuition, always. May you honour your natural rhythms and live inspired and aligned lives. May you be deeply loved and nourished by those you hold dear.

I see my role in your lives as one of love, guidance, and protection. You are my greatest gifts.

I love you.

xx

INTRODUCTION

Our wisdom and what we 'know' changes as we grow. From conception onwards, we are in a constant state of change and personal growth. In the early years, our physical growth captivates. The whole world astounded by the way kids 'grow so quickly.'

Our children come to this world complete, yet rarely are they seen this way. We've become obsessed with the great race.

Racing to grow kids up.

Relentlessly pursuing the next milestone, from birth.

Pushing our young towards the next big achievement, scoring, and categorising them along the way.

Expecting children to be tiny versions of adults even when the brain research and lived experience of families worldwide screams, 'Stop, it's too much, too fast!'

Our kids don't come to this world to be entered into the great race. They simply arrive and find themselves amongst it, absorbing and assimilating, through osmosis.

What if I told you the big race was all a lie, a distraction and detraction from the true gift of life? What would your lived experience be if your family chose not to enter you into the great race when you were small?

How would our world be different if we decided not to enter our kids into the great race of life? Can you see it?

I see a world where going slow is revered, where rhythms are honoured, and children are gifted with permission to show up as they are.

After all, children are equipped with all they need to explore what's meaningful to them, moment by moment. The big race is a mystery to our kids until we condition and program them otherwise.

Busy isn't in a child's repertoire, until we put it there.

So let's not put it there in the first place.

We've got a personal development industry and a myriad of modalities helping people reconnect to self. Programs, courses, resources, memberships, masterminds and 10 step plans all centred around reconnecting you to you!

But when we were kids, we knew. We were connected.

That's the first thing I want you to know.

You Already Knew.

Kids know how to be kids.

Adolescents know how to be adolescents.

Adults, in theory, should kind of remember what it's like to be both. But we don't, we forget, and so we don't treat kids the way we wanted to be treated. We treat them how we were treated. We indoctrinate them into the pursuit of the next big thing. And so, the great race continues.

Adults unable to slow down enough to play fail to adequately advocate for a child's right to play. Play is a fundamental basic human right, it ought not need advocating for.

As we move through life and come to know more about the great race, our creativity dulls and takes a back seat to more 'important things.'

Unbridled joy becomes a thing of the past, from the good old days.

What was once known becomes that of a bygone era. What's 'known' by adulthood is all a bit too serious, a bit too busy, and a bit too centred around 'work' for my liking.

Before long, we get good at that too. We focus on our output, the work that we do. Ever found yourself in this situation?

You bump into someone you haven't seen for a while. You exchange pleasantries like you've been socialised and programmed to do. Directly after you've greeted the race of who has been the most busy begins.

"How have you been?"

"So busy, it's been hectic really."

"Yeah, me too. I've been so busy."

And the great race is on. Who will win?

Who has been the busiest?

Who has successfully burnt themselves out in the great race of life?

The brief encounter comes to an end, likely abruptly.

"Anyway, I better get going. So much to do."

As you walk away, you tally the score. You've either won and are the victor as the most worn-down, burnt-out person.

Or worse, you realise you haven't been anywhere near as busy as that person and make a commitment to pick up your pace.

Couldn't be seen to be doing nothing after all....

As a result of the way we were raised and the examples we've observed for a lifetime, we tend to conform to the rules of the game.

This is adulting. Before long this becomes our life and our identity,

busy.

We leave who we were and what we knew behind for who we are told to be, and what we are told to know.

Parenthood sees us smacked in the face with childhood again. Only we are now the big people. A second opportunity to experience childhood as we witness its magic through the eyes of our child.

But do we take it up?

Do we see it as a gift?

Do we recognise the innate wisdom of our children, from birth?

I've found that unless we commit to stepping out of the great race to witness the magic of childhood, the experience is not nearly as fun.

After all, having tiny people in the home is unproductive. Your capacity to do all the things is severely impacted. But, on the upside, you usually win the 'so busy' conversations nowadays. And you get to pop a side of 'on very little sleep' into your story for dramatic effect.

Where is the line between who you were, who you are and who you are yet to become? There is none.

Yes, there are defining moments and milestones along the way in life, but you are the same soul you were when you entered this world. Your purpose, worth, and capacity for growth have been there from the very start.

As we grow and navigate the transitions of our lives, our values shift, our perceptions shift, and as a result, our actions change. With this book, it is my hope that you rediscover and connect to what is profoundly purposeful and soul aligned for you. I want you to give yourself permission to go slow as you absorb the words on these pages. Give yourself permission to go slow and soak it in.

Allow me to mosey with you as you journey through the experiences of your life, look inward introspectively, and choose your path forward. I intentionally chose the word 'mosey' here instead of 'walk'. To walk is to 'move at a regular pace by lifting and setting down each foot in turn.'

To mosey is to 'move in a leisurely manner.' This tiny language shift helps orient me towards the spiritual practice of going slower, seeing the race, and choosing not to get caught up in the crowd. I'm not here to race for the finish line. I choose to be here, with me, with you, with my children in the reality we call the present. The question is, where are you?

It is my hope that you find flow and an increased capacity to mosey alongside your children. As a person who has invested an exorbitant amount of energy into slowing down, I see it as an extraordinary gift to raise children who know slow, who grow up with the blueprint for how to move in a leisurely manner.

There are no "10 steps to parenthood happiness," no one size fits all approach that'll see you thrive.

One thing I know to be true though is this.

You Already Knew.
No matter the question.
No matter the obstacle.
No matter the fear.

You Already Knew. And if you knew, then it means you still know.

If ever you are in doubt about what to do, I ask that you look to your child. Look to your child as the authority, they know who they are and what they need. Our kids hold an ancient wisdom. The answers you seek are here.

As you navigate the pages of this book I ask that you consider how what I present here applies to your life. I have come to understand that parenting is an act of surrender. As we travel through the experiences of your life and look at the ways your childhood has shaped you, I invite you to come back to that. "Parenting as an act of surrender."

In the practice of parenting, we must become adept at pausing, pondering, and pivoting. To do so requires surrender.

If we hold onto how it 'should' be (rigidity), we are robbed of joy. If we lose our footing and get swept out into the sea of emotions (chaos), we rob ourselves of the beauty and wisdom of our existence.

So how do we unpick and unravel the stories of our lives and the meaning we've attached to them through the art and practice of parenting?

We surrender.

We live each day, in that day, for that day, in the relationship of family.

When we meet our kid's needs they come to understand that they are heard. When children feel heard they are loving, aware, present, open, connected, and they want to contribute.

When we meet our kid's needs they rest easy, a deep calm contentment visible in their bodies when they sleep. It's beautiful to witness and, I've found, gives insight into how our kids are feeling. So pause a moment and get a felt sense for how your kids are travelling by witnessing their sleep.

I believe it to be our natural state to sleep this way, yet it's quite uncommon for us as adults. When is the last time you found that exceptionally comfortable position and drifted off to sleep in devine comfort free of stress, worry, or urgency about what still needs to be 'done?' Young children are masterful at it. It's why your kids will wriggle and writhe, get in and out of bed 15 times to gather pillows and blankets and soft things only to pile them up into a nest.

Often we big people feel our energy rising when in close proximity to it, the constant moving and adjusting and rearranging of the space threatening to overwhelm our nervous system. Our programming and conditioning tell us that we must lie down and go to sleep quickly and without a fuss. But what if we were to approach going off to sleep like a small person? What if we committed to finding that divinely comfortable position? What would it shift for us?

Throughout this book, I'll mention and reference terms such as child, children, kids. I'm speaking here interchangeably about our world's most precious resource, children.

I'll also reference mum, mother, motherhood, mothering and parenting. I am speaking from my experience as a white woman in a heterosexual relationship. It is my hope that you can modify my language to match your experience, preferred pronoun and identity.

You'll find that I've also omitted several words as much as possible in my writing too. This is an intentional choice and extends beyond the pages of this book.

I believe language to be potent and as such I'm mindful of the words and terms I choose to use both here as we explore what You Already Knew and in my daily life as a mother, wife, and child activist. In this book, you won't find me making mention of;

Learning – I'll use growth, absorption, or osmosis.

Teach – I'll use share or facilitate

Busy – I'll use a range of other less urgent or rushed language choices, including terms like priorities or resources.

Time – I'll speak of investment, energy or resources.

Work – I'll speak of contribution or exploration.

I'll also avoid terms such as good work, good boy/girl, and be careful in this book in the same way I avoid their use in my day-to-day life.

We'll delve into why further in chapter eight - words matter. I wanted to bring your awareness to it now so that you can see how language shifts matter along the way.

We are going to explore concepts in this book that are at odds with the dominant narrative, likely at odds with how you were raised and at times you may find yourself experiencing a visceral response to the ideas and perception shifts I am putting forward.

These are the moments to get still and quiet, to get curious about why. Where did it come from? Who's belief is it? Does it serve you? Is there another way? What FEELS soul aligned?

This journey asks you to get really clear about what you believe, who you are and how you show up in the world.

We are all living our own unique experiences. I believe no one person's experience is more or less valid because of their identity, culture, beliefs, or values. I see you in your experience, I accept you as you are, and I value your voice.

I'd love to connect with you further on your journey. There are some ways at the back of the book to connect with me, I would love to hear your voice and understand your lived experience. I believe we can heal the collective hurts of the world through sharing our stories and hearing the voices of others. Please come and find me. I'd love to connect with you.

This book is filled with the experiences of my life, the lessons and gifts I've picked up along the way. Many of the stories I will share have had a profound impact on how I do life and how I see children.

Throughout this book, you'll find three common threads.

Relationship

Intuition

Trust

It is my hope that through bathing in the energy of this book, you deepen your relationships, extend your intuition, and grow your trust. For I believe it is through the reclamation of what we already knew that we can find solutions to the questions we ask. The answers aren't as straightforward as a set of rigid steps. The solution comes through introspection, through knowing yourself and what you already knew.

In doing so you'll naturally make different choices. Your relationships, intuition, and trust in yourself will morph and you'll find your family flow. I am here to mosey with you while you remember, while you reclaim your truth.

Reclamation of your innate childhood wisdom is not about looking back, it's about bringing forth.

Let's explore what You Already Knew.

SECTION ONE

SOLID FOUNDATION

CHAPTER ONE

HUMAN-BEING

We've all got one thing in common. Can you guess what it is?

It's simple.

When you go beyond all the ways in which we differ, beyond the ways we categorise and sort ourselves, there's one common thread that connects us all.

We are all human.

Regardless of race, culture, gender, spiritual belief, or age, we are all humans sharing the human experience on this planet.

When you strip away all of the constructs we've created, I believe every single person on this planet is equally valuable and should be treated as such. This includes children. Yet this is not what I've witnessed.

We all entered the world dependent upon the adults around us. Born as human infants requiring the nurturance and support of adults. We are a species with highly dependent young. We have the longest period of growth from infancy to maturation in the animal world. Our young are vulnerable, there are no two ways about it. What infancy looks like in the animal kingdom is as varied and unique as the diversity of species themselves.

From the Orangutan with the longest childhood dependence, after us, of any animal in the world, to reptiles who rarely have anything to do with their young. Imagine for a moment the concept of birthing young independent enough that they require nothing from you, from birth.

Orangutan babies nurse until they are about six years of age and remain with their mothers for several years after. Female orangutans are longer still to develop mothering skills through observation. Snakes aren't vulnerable. They like many reptiles, are born with the ability to take care of themselves.

Our babies can't do those things. Our babies need us.

As I see it, the problem is that this very vulnerability often frames the way children are seen by adults.

Children viewed as incapable, incomplete or inadequate.

Children perceived as unable to be trusted, incapable of meaningful involvement.

Children considered unworthy until they mature, grow up, earn the right to be called' adults.'

As a result, adults often fail to consult children on matters that affect them. Do you remember how that felt?

I do.

It hurt.

If you've picked up this book, you've likely reached the age where you've been given that title.

Adult.

What if I told you that you had it right when you were small, that how you saw the world held, in part, the keys to your parenting success? What would it look like for you to reclaim your childhood wisdom?

Let's explore that together.

For each lap around the sun you've done you've taken in information and data. You've processed it, stored some, and it's all shaped the way you do life. You are a product of your environment and lived experiences.

You have unique synaptic superhighways in your brain. They've been laid down through the sum of your life's experiences. Yet none of your most recent experiences have had nearly the impact upon your brain as those that occurred early in your life. We know that the early years are important. I'm willing to say that we still have much to understand about just how critical the early years are.

Yet if you travel back through your life to your childhood and do a bit of investigation, you'll find the you that you once knew. What are the stories of your childhood? How do others describe the child version of you? Have you paused to consider how the stories of your childhood inform your truth? When I reflect upon the way I was described as a child there are similarities and striking differences between accounts. What we have here is perception, the lens through which each person sees the world.

Coming to understand this led me to look a little deeper for my core truth. In reviewing photos from my childhood, I was able to gain a clearer picture of self. Instead of just looking at photos for a moment I sat with them a little longer. Asking myself if I could remember the photo being taken, recalling any memories, and seeking to gain a felt sense of self through the way I held my body or the look on my face.

It was an incredibly insightful experience that solidified to me that who I am, at my core is who I have always been. I'd simply steered off the path a little as I came to be who I thought the world needed me to be.

You are as unique as your most striking features, as interesting as your laugh. Yes, we all have our humanity in common, but how we live, think, act, and experience LIFE are uniquely ours.

You are an extraordinarily unique being. No one shares your views, experiences, priorities, values, beliefs, or transgenerational inheritance.

You are an extraordinarily unique being indeed.

But how much focus and energy do you dedicate to being?

Being in the moment?

Being attuned to your needs and those of your children?

Being connected to those you love?

Being connected to the land?

Being authentically and unapologetically you?

Being still?

Are you a **Human-being**, or are you in a perpetual cycle of **Human-doing**?

Doing all of the things.

Doing what you've been conditioned to do.

Doing what you perceive to be the right thing?

Doing,

Doing,

Doing to the point of exhaustion and burnout?

Doing anything you can to get to the end of your to-do list so you can feel accomplished enough just to BE?

If that induces pain, guilt or shame, please know this is not my intention. However, this realisation needs to be uncomfortable enough to get you to move, or even better, be still.

Pain is feedback to get us to create change, so if this is painful to ponder, your body is giving you feedback for you to shift, pivot, and design a life more congruent to human-being. True freedom in your human experience lies in your capacity to be.

In my experience, the humans who are the most proficient at BEING are the small ones. Children are experts at it.

Children aren't trying to get through the to-do list of life first.

Children aren't drawing a line between their capacity to do all of the things and their worth.

Children aren't focussed on doing all of the things before they are allowed to be.

Busy isn't in a child's repertoire, until we put it there.

What children are DOING is showing us what it is to simply BE. But that depends on our capacity to see. Can you see it? Can you see how your kids lead you towards a greater capacity to be? If not, let me put it to you this way.

Have you ever found yourself so caught up in play that time simply slipped away, ceased to exist? The kind of situation where you end up being late, but it was totally worth it. No regrets.

Have you experienced a level of joy and connection so deep you forgot to DO the things on your list?

If so, you've been dealt a lesson directly from the child's playbook of life. A dose of human-being wrapped up in 'play.'

Right after you were gifted that experience, you likely found yourself 'falling behind' the timeline you'd set yourself. You may have felt like you were now going to be chasing your tail. You may even have thought you'd 'wasted' valuable time you could have used to DO something.

Where did you pick that up along the way? This might have happened for you right around the stage you started doing 'homework.'

It's a trap. I'm here to tell you that this pattern of thinking is a trap! A trap to keep you fighting against the clock and in a perpetual cycle of human-doing.

Resist it.

Resist and reject the conditioning that says your worth lies in your capacity to do!

Your genius lies in your capacity to balance out DOING and BEING. Doing is easy for us adults. It's being that can be tricky. Knowing where to start, in my experience, is where the challenge lies. How does one make the shifts necessary to go from human-doing to human BEING?

You play.

When we play, we be.

It's that simple. Once we know the way to 'be', the question shifts from how to where! So, where do you feel most at ease playing?

At the beach?

Down at the park?

In a pillow fort in your pyjamas?

If you've forgotten, that's ok. Cast your eye back to your childhood. Where did you play? Where did you go when you needed a break from the world?

If you feel like you need a break from the world now, you have likely tipped the scales a little too far into the doing. Go back to the beginning of your play career. All you need to know lies there.

Our society largely fails to value play, and I believe it's because play is not perceived as achieving anything as determined by societies rules. It has no place in the adult realm. So, play is demonised, or worse, it is given status and meaning by calling it a 'child's work.'

Play is not a child's work.
Play is a fundamental human right.

The role and benefits of play extend well beyond childhood. You may have achieved the title of adult. This in and of itself does not signify the end of your playing career.

You haven't lost the human-being capacity, the capacity for play. When you were a child, you knew how to play. You knew how to be. You Already Knew. You can reconnect to you, the childlike you of the past and bring forth your wisdom. You can merge and consolidate all of who you are to be whole in your human experience.

If you've picked up this book, you are likely a parent or a person who spends a lot of time with children. You are also likely to be a person who views children as capable.

Whether you are spending your day supporting and guiding your children or the children of others, I want you to know that what you do matters! The way children feel in your presence, alongside all the tasks you do with and for them are of value.

I want you to remember it's not always about 'doing the things.' Often the most important 'thing' hasn't a thing to do with doing. It's BEING.

Being present in the moment, where your feet are, being with what is and delighting in the small human-being in front of you.

Through relationship and connection with children, you can reconnect to yourself AND gift children the blueprint for a connected life.

Connected.

In the moment.

At ease.

Peaceful.

Tranquil.

Relaxed.

All of these are states of BEING. Yeah?

Being, not doing.

So, I ask you this. If you quit DOING the things for a day, if you were to stop with the relentless pursuit of the to-do list, what would human-being look like for you?

If you allowed yourself to be led by the wisdom of your inner child, what would be the story of your life?

What would you do?

Where would you go?

Who would be around?

Who would you BE?

Have you the courage to let it all fly by the wayside and live out that reality today? If so, please do. You'll fast track your capacity to BE and develop the capacity to balance out the BEING and the DOING much quicker. The shift requires a commitment to unlearning that which has been conditioned. That which has been indoctrinated. That which has been passed onto you, often unintentionally.

If it all seems a bit much. If the weight and pressure of your to-do list feel too big, If even the thought of BEING today instead of DOING induces fear or panic, please simply take a moment to daydream about what Human-being for a day would look like. Daydream about who you would be if you were simply to BE.

Let's take this book, for example. You Already Knew came through me during a season of life where I could have easily been focussed on DOING all of the things. This book came through me in our son's first year of life. A year that often saw me isolated and carrying the mental load of parenting alone. A year that saw us relocate across the country and navigate some immense challenges as a family.

So here I was, alone but not alone in the intensity of supporting Wahri through his first year of life. Yet the writing of this book has been easeful. It has flowed. I've been able to BE here, in a state of book writing. I've remained open and allowed the words to pour forth. This book, these words are the culmination of my life's experiences, my life's gifts and my life's lessons to date.

To me, the art of BEING does not mean getting nothing done. It's a practice and an energetic shift in how you do life. It's noticing the nuance between done with love and done out of obligation, don't forget the side of resentment served up with the latter. It's the difference between honouring your natural rhythm and pushing on at all costs.

It has set me free to recognise that the doing can happen as a result of being. You might think you aren't doing anything when you play with your kids, but the gift of your presence and your capacity to be with them is everything to your child.

You'll ebb and flow as you bring your awareness to a shift from human-doing to human-being. You'll have days where you nail it and days where you fall well short. This is normal.

It's more about the energetic shift and a capacity to change gears, dial down, and get into the flow state of BEING. It's a practice, one I focus on every day.

I've spent much more of my life as a human-doing than a human-being. It wasn't until I saw how this pattern was playing out in my life and robbing me of joy that I was able to do life differently. And you can too.

All my life I've been described as a 'goer' or a 'hard worker'. Accolades for working myself to the bone, soldiering on regardless of my level of burnout and sticking to the thing. Seeing it through NO MATTER WHAT worn like a badge of honour. Look at me go, I can do all of the things. Cue Beyoncé's track 'Independent Woman!'

When my now husband and I were dating, he would call me out on my human-doing identity and relentless pursuit of independence by saying, 'Righto

Beyoncé, you've got those independent woman vibes coming through.'

He was lovingly and with humour inviting me to see where I was being rigidly independent. He was inviting me to soften, to shift gears and get out of my own way. Now I must mention that my Husband Brendan has an exceptional capacity to be. You'll find him living his best life out bush following his natural rhythms and taking cues from the land. I've gained so much of what I now know to be true about being through observation and osmosis from him.

Anyway, back to being Beyoncé. "No, we don't need to do the lawns while you are home this weekend. I can get it done through the week. I'll find time!"

"I'll swing past the shops and get the food organised for camping on my lunch break and have the car packed when you finish work so we can get on the road."

You see, I am an expert at cramming the most amount of DOING into the smallest pockets of time. It's a game of Tetris to me, and I love Tetris. Efficient and effective, that's me.

It was my mantra.

Efficient and effective. I made for an ideal employee. I'd take on all of the things and do whatever it took to get the job done, at all costs.

Through the rejection of support, I kept myself in the role of human-doing. I didn't have TIME to sit still, to stop. I was not at all open to accepting help. To ask for help was to fail. To admit defeat. Right?

So here's the thing, when we are rigidly independent, it takes away our opportunity to be in relationship and community. It takes away our opportunity to receive.

Pretty soon, we tell ourselves a story that it can't get done unless we do it, we tell ourselves that no one else will help, and then we find evidence to support that truth. It's called confirmation bias and we all do it.

In my work, home, and relationships, I was saying to the world, "I've got this. I'm tired. I'm run down and exhausted. But I'm committed to my identity as a human-doing."

Until...

Until I found myself experiencing an increasing number of seemingly unrelated symptoms and complaints, I was falling apart. Things were not going well. And I was in my early 30's.

How did I get here?

Where was I headed?

How could I turn it around?

There had to be an answer. A REASON for why I was falling apart. If only I could find it!

Cue a frantic up levelling of the already lightning speed game of Tetris. I was now relentless in my pursuit of answers.

It turns out I was my own worst enemy. My relentless doing was my core problem. The rest of the symptoms were simply collateral damage. Coming to this realisation was like

hitting

a

brick

wall.

My entire identity and the way I showed up in the world was built around my output, what I could DO.

Without that identity, who was I?

Without that identity, was I worthy?

Without that identity, what would my life look like?

Just as the space between the drumbeat gives the sound its power, I was being invited to slow the beat of my life, to lengthen out the moments of silence and stillness.

It was a terrifying concept. How could I be expected to STOP doing all of the things? I was burnt out enough from all of the things. Now you mean to tell me I need to schedule in NOT doing things? I won't have the capacity to sleep. I'm too busy to slow down! It's not possible! Sound familiar?

Once I had come to terms with what I needed to do, which was less about doing and more about being, I began the journey of healing my body, quieting my mind (still my biggest challenge), and flexing my human-being muscle.

As I healed, I began to see the world anew. I began to see my own experiences through a new lens and moved steadily towards my true purpose. I shifted my perceptions around who I am in the world and the contributions I make.

I changed my mind about having a baby. I'd been involved in the lives of children all my life. I'd been doing life believing I couldn't support the world's children and raise my own. I simply couldn't see a reality with children of my own before I healed. In hindsight, it's part of why I put so much effort into providing a wholesome environment and opportunities for the children of others. You see, for me, that was simple. I could do that. I was clever enough to work myself to the bone chasing what I desired for the world's children. Freedom.

I recall even telling people who would inevitably ask me when I was having children that I wouldn't be able to serve the children of the world and raise my own. I had perceived myself to be so busy that it was a 'this or that' situation. I believed I had to choose.

As I began to slow down. As I learnt to be, I saw that I could do both. Ironically the key to my doing of both was in my capacity to be.

Fast forward a couple of years to the conscious conception, pregnancy and planned freebirth of our son Wahri. This is where I found myself in the spiritual practice of surrender, going slow, and being completely connected to my body and our baby. I finally got it, I finally got what being a human-being was all about. Here it finally was, my point of reference for what it feels like to BE. It's a glorious thing.

The journey to Wahri's birth was transformative. I was entirely at home in my body throughout my pregnancy, I was at ease, peaceful, and felt deeply connected to our unborn child. The synchronicity experienced throughout my pregnancy was only equalled by his birth.

At the time of writing this chapter, Wahri was nine months old, and I can feel the distance travelled on my journey to human-being. I can see how this pathway was carved out FOR me. I can see how my life experiences have set me up for my present reality and future direction.

Each occasion where I've wandered off the path has served me. I can see that now. I can see how I continue to grow as I navigate the dance between doing and being.

I can see how my children and the children of the world guide and hold me accountable to the daily spiritual practice of human-being.

You may not remember what it feels like to be, but the you of years gone by does. I share my experience with you to serve as a guidepost and an example of one person's journey. This dance between doing and being has made an immense difference to my daily experience.

CHAPTER TWO

VALUES

We each live our lives by a set of priorities, things that are important to us. These are called our values. Your lived experience has shaped them, and here's the interesting thing. It's a co-creation, your values shape your lived experience as much as your lived experience shapes your values. Make sense?

In every moment of every day, we are taking in, analysing, and making meaning from the experiences of our lives. Our brains take in over 10 billion bits of data every second! This is well beyond what we can handle, let alone process. We're consciously aware of less than 1%

of what comes our way. Less than 1%, does that make anyone else cringe about all the essential things they've missed in the other 99?

There's simply more coming at us than we can process. And so, we filter. We filter what comes in so that we can, hopefully, process what's most important for us.

Ever turned down the volume on the car stereo when driving on unfamiliar roads?

Ever found yourself closing your eyes so you can hear that strange sound in the distance clearer?

You are filtering.

We filter and curate our lived experiences based on our values, priorities, and worldview. It is my belief that when we find ourselves frustrated, irritated, or disconnected there's often an aspect of our values that is not in alignment.

Freedom is one of my highest values. I seek it constantly. Things don't tend to well for me when my sense of freedom is being threatened.

I recall a period in my life when my sense of freedom felt very threatened. I'd been through an all-consuming relationship breakdown, and my life had shifted direction significantly from where I 'thought' it was going.

At that stage, I perceived this to be a bad thing. It wasn't. It was the shift that put me onto my true path. I simply didn't know it yet. I'd been living a life that was not aligned with my highest values.

So here I was, alone and floundering. Wondering who I was, what I believed, what this meant for the life I had been living and for the life I would carry on to live. Things were not going well for me.

But I had my dog, and I had my 4wd. My 4wd became my freedom on four wheels. I could go anywhere I chose and get far enough away from the noise of the world to hear my inner guidance.

Until.... Inevitably, it broke. That'll happen when you've got a highly modified vehicle over 20 years old.

It broke, and I panicked. Suddenly my freedom on four wheels couldn't take me anywhere, it needed to be repaired, and I wasn't confident I knew how.

It turns out a perceived lack of freedom can be pretty motivating to me, I set to task gaining the skills necessary to fix my car, and when that engine roared, I could feel the freedom coursing through my veins. I had gained a newfound sense of freedom.

Once I figured out that my 4wd signified freedom on four wheels, I could see how a perceived lack of freedom was playing out in my life.

I still felt my heart begin to race, and a mild panic start to take hold when something happened to my beloved old 4wd, but I was beginning to understand that it was less about the car and more about freedom. Fast forward to my lived experience of writing this book, and I found myself being gifted the opportunity to once again recalibrate my perception of freedom.

A cross country adventure to relocate our family from the Northern Territory to Queensland began with my old 4wd loaded up as the tow vehicle. My freedom on four wheels charged with securing safe passage for all our worldly belongings.

Only that's not how it played out. A catastrophic engine failure stopped her dead in her tracks.

How would I feel?

How would I respond?

And what would I do when faced with the reality of the situation?

There was no mild panic, no scarcity, as I heard my husband call out, 'We've got some dramas' over the UHF as he brought the whole show to a halt. I pulled over and knew instantly by the lack of a running engine, we were indeed in trouble. The old girl had shut herself down. She'd ended her journey and asked us to adjust our expectations, pivot our plans, and turn problems into possibilities.

As I stood in the 37 Degree Celsius afternoon heat swaying with our nine month old on my hip, I saw the end of an era. I didn't crumple. I didn't panic. I simply smiled. I saw myself in all the panicked predicaments of the past, and I smiled with a knowing that I had transcended. Transcended the version of myself who held such tight control in order to maintain a sense of safety. Transcended the need for my freedom to come from outside of me. I was ready to let her go. I was free.

Each time I recount this story I find myself overwhelmed with emotion. That old car was so important to me for so long. I'd joked about never selling it, and when I'd received offers, I declined such a ludicrous idea, fiercely. And you know what, I wasn't wrong. It wasn't for sale, and I was destined not to sell it, ever. Instead, I gifted it to a young fellow in the hope that he would find the drive and motivation to give her yet another life.

You see, I now have a point of reference for true freedom. I have a lived experience affirming I've got freedom, and I rest easy in that knowledge. Old 4wd or not, it's there, and for someone who values freedom so deeply, it's rather freeing to know. You know?

Since coming to understand my values on a deep level, I can cultivate my life in ways that align with my high value on freedom. Freedom is essential for my husband, too. The opportunity to freely choose how and where he invests his energy and resources fuels many of his decisions. Freedom is one of our core values and as a result influences our parenting decisions and actions. We will get to how in the coming chapters, for now the most important thing to know is that freedom is also important for our children. Is it any surprise given that they are being raised in a home where freedom is a core value?

For my stepdaughter Hailey, freedom comes from being consulted and included in decision making. She thrives on being asked to share her opinions and views. For Wahri, free movement is of the utmost importance. Anything he perceives as caging or restricting his movements is met with frustration or fear. Wahri has also cultivated a strong capacity to communicate and simply does not accept the widely held notion of adults that babies have nothing valuable to say or contribute. Wahri invests resources into the acquisition of language, well beyond that of his developmental age and as such, he demands to be heard and understood. What a beautiful thing! With the knowledge of what freedom looks like for each of us in mind, we can navigate the experiences of our lives as a family.

Understanding your values and cultivating a life that supports them is life changing, but seeing and honing your child in their values is entirely different.

In what ways do your kid's highest values play out?

Are you able to see your child through their highest values?

Your child's values are going to challenge you, you may even find they trigger. When this happens, I have found that the value is either too close or too far away from a value you hold. If there's something your kid loves that irritates you no end, you've found it!

What then?

What do you do when your child's values are at odds with your own?

In my experience, it's not so much about what you do. It's more about remaining open. By remaining open, you'll start to see things differently. That thing that irritates you no end becomes an entry point to deeper understanding and connection. Because here's the thing, we don't have to feel a full body yes about all the things the people we live with love. We can love them while not loving that thing they do.

Our children's values serve and offer growth opportunities to us, always.

It may take a little while to uncover your child's highest values, but you will be well equipped to speak to them in their values once you do. You'll be communicating that you understand them and affirming for them that what they value is important to you. Heard, your kids will feel heard. Do you remember what it felt like when you were heard as a child?

Speaking to children about values is profoundly beautiful. In our home, conversations about values are commonplace. I recall one of the first explicit values conversations my husband Brendan and I had with Hailey. She was recounting to us some of the differences between her two family homes. We could see her dancing with the desire to remain loyal to both while becoming entangled in how that could be possible in a world of opposites.

We big people are experts at conditioning children to recognise pairs and opposites.

Yes – No.

Good – Bad.

Right – Wrong.

Nice – Mean.

Fun – Boring.

Love – Hate.

We start subtly in the early years, and before long, we've created a lens for our children to view the world through. One where they are constantly seeking to categorise and judge things by the predetermined rules of the game. Is it any wonder Hailey was grappling with what this meant for her?

After expressing to Hailey our belief that it didn't need to be a 'one is right, and one is wrong' situation, we shifted the focus to values by asking Hailey to describe what each parent valued, how they choose to spend their time, what they each like to do. Hailey listed off what her mum and dad each liked to do. Afterwards we helped her see the similarities. There weren't many. We spoke of the differences. There were plenty.

From this place, Hailey was able to see how this wasn't a one is right, and one is wrong situation. She understood that she didn't need to feel like a traitor to her mother when she was here with us. Nor was she a traitor to her father when she was with her mum.

Navigating vastly different values and belief structures is challenging, especially for our kids. If we are to set them up for success, we must be truthful. We must be open. I believe that when our children know we are trustworthy and that we are willing to navigate the tricky bits with them, everybody wins.

We could have simply 'told' Hailey that it's okay to have different homes, and she may have taken solace and possibly even believed us, for a while.

Instead, we chose to open a dialogue with her that gives her the tools to see and speak to people in their values. Since this first values conversation, Hailey often speaks with us about her shifting and emerging values or the values of others.

These conversations support Hailey to understand better what drives people's perceptions, decisions, and actions.

So how do you gain a deeper understanding of your child's values?

Where do you even start? Great question!

You start by getting curious.

Pondering the following questions may assist you in understanding your child's values.

What is your child's eye drawn towards?

How does your child fill their space?

What is intolerable to your child?

What triggers you the most about your child?

Let's look at some of Wahri's highest values at the time of writing this chapter. Wahri Jay Haack - 11 months.

What is your child's eye drawn towards?

Wahri has a lot of language, his capacity for communication has been evident from birth. He is often described as an 'old soul' and consistently captivates strangers in the street. As he grows and gains more words, he's adept at pulling them out at precisely the right moment to elicit a response. He's got a lot to say, and he delights in conversation, the entirely present kind with all the eye contact. He will cut the conversation short if he suspects you aren't fully present.

He is also consistently drawn toward wheels and anything that goes around. He can spot a set of wheels anywhere, and he must investigate them. Pushing things along while carefully observing the moving parts is a must.

How does your child fill their space?

At the present moment, everything must be out. Things contained inside other things is no good. It's got to be out where you can see it, touch it, feel it and experience it. Hello Schema play!

What is intolerable to your child?

Above all else, Wahri finds being confined intolerable. This is closely followed by trying to communicate to an adult who is either missing the point or choosing not to pick up what he is putting down. These two things are sure to elicit a response that communicates his distaste. Hi there freedom!

What triggers you the most about your child?

I've come to understand that freedom plus freedom doesn't equal more freedom. If I am not feeling free and Wahri brings me a need for more freedom, this can be challenging for me. It's a clear indicator that I need to shift something to feel like I'm doing life aligned with my high value on freedom when his need for freedom rubs me up the wrong way.

CHAPTER THREE

BELIEFS

In the last chapter, we looked at how our values influence our perceptions, decisions, and actions. We also sought to gain a deeper understanding of our children's values and how to get everyone's needs met in the family unit. Our values are however not solely responsible for how we experience life. Within us also lay belief structures, largely laid down in early childhood.

A vast majority of the things you believe to be true may be nothing more than the beliefs of others that have been gifted to you when your brain was being built. For most of us, we make it through to adulthood, and often much further, without ever pausing to ponder if what we believe to be true is truth. To put it nicely, what we believe to be true is a complex and convoluted mess.

As children, we were conditioned to seek out and identify opposites. Many of the beliefs we hold as adults result from the programming and conditioning of our childhood.

So, if many of the things you believe to be true are beliefs that were gifted to you, how do you work out what's yours and what's not?

Where is the threshold between what you believe to be true and what you've been told to believe is true?

What truths are your own, and which have you picked up along the way without realising?

And how one earth are you supposed to know the difference between the two?

If you've wondered these things, you are not alone. These questions come up for many people around the same time they decide to be parents.

The answer is simple yet complex. We are seeking to make the unconscious conscious here, and it starts with curiosity.

If you choose to pivot and change the way you do life, I want you to know this choice will likely be met with resistance.

Through transforming your beliefs, you'll trigger. So, if you've already triggered people, keep going!

By dissolving the way 'it's always been' and choosing to go a different way, you'll divide. Do it anyway, keep going!

When you remove the barriers of your mind, you'll remember who you are. Keep going!

You'll be unrecognisable, and that'll unnerve some. And that is completely ok. I'd rather run the risk of disappointing someone close to me than live a life ruled by the beliefs of others. To me, that's an unacceptable life path, one I won't stand for.

Making the unconscious conscious requires a commitment to being curious about what you believe and asking yourself simple questions. You can do that by asking yourself these simple questions whenever you notice you've got a belief.

Why do I believe that?

Where did it come from?

What do I believe to be true?

When you notice a belief come up, it's an invitation to get curious.

Now I realise that what I am putting forward here is in stark contrast to how most of us were raised. After all, the concepts explored in this book are quite the opposite of behaviourism.

Up until recently, behaviourism has been the core tenet of mainstream parenting and it is entirely possible that you, like me, have behaviourism parenting traits that surface from time to time.

If you find yourself gravitating toward having 'power over' children in times of stress or discomfort (read: misbehaviour) you might hold a core belief that a human's true nature is bad. And here's the thing, if that's what you were shown as a child, if that was your lived experience it makes sense that on a cellular level you carry that with you. You absorbed that 'truth' through osmosis. Belief!

If having power over children doesn't resonate with you this is an opportunity to dissolve the core behaviourist approach beliefs that you were handed as a child. Let's look at some other commonly held beliefs from the bygone era of behaviourism.

When children behave in ways that adults 'want' the child is responded to with attention and rewards. Conversely when children behave in ways that adults don't want the child is responded to with a withdrawal of love or punishment. It is seen as our role, as adults, to teach children how to behave appropriately, by whatever means 'necessary.'

Let's look a little closer. Punishment is defined as 'the infliction or imposition of a penalty as retribution for an offence.' Through a behaviourist lens, this must commence from birth. If a human's true nature is bad, then we must begin with punishment immediately.

"Put that baby down" - she needs to learn to self-settle.

"He's having a meltdown" - he needs to learn that he can't get his own way.

"Give the toy to your brother" - she needs to learn to share.

"Stop complaining" - he needs to learn that the world doesn't revolve around him.

Now here's the thing. If what we desire is for our children to develop the capacity for self-regulation, for compassion, to connect with and cooperate with others. If we intend for them to recognise that they fit within this infinitely interconnected community we call life on earth, do we really think we will get there through blame, shame, coercion, and control? Will a behaviourist approach laced with punishment and archaic 'teaching' yield that result? I think not, and you'll not convince me, nor science otherwise.

There's a name for the blame, shame, coercion and control of friends, family, and random strangers in the street, gaslighting. In the words of Elyse Myers, "I don't receive that." You are under absolutely no obligation to receive gaslighting wrapped up neatly as sound parenting advice.

There's a difference between hearing and embodying such unsolicited advice. It cannot affect you if you are able to see it for what it is. What you have is a person standing in front of you gifting you with some insight into their world view which includes their values, beliefs and lived experience. When I am offered unsolicited advice, I listen carefully.

I am listening for the fundamental core beliefs of the person speaking to me. I am seeking to understand their world view and their words are giving me an insight into their mind. When they are done, I thank them for sharing what they believe to be true. Sometimes I will offer them some context around my perceptions, decisions, and actions not because I am trying to justify myself but because I desire to see a world where adults are perceiving, deciding, and acting from a place of alignment, not automation.

I come back to alignment over automation a lot. When Hailey was four, she recounted a story from her day that held a scientific element. Upon asking her some open-ended questions, she looked me square in the eyes and asked, "Zo, do you already know about this?" To which I responded that I knew a few things about it. I told her I was interested in understanding what she knew.

This didn't cut it with her, she quickly turned the open-ended questioning back on me, and I found myself having questions fired at me quicker than I could answer them. When her thirst to find out what I 'knew' was satiated, she said, "Zo, you are so smart. You could be a science when you grow up." (Science meaning scientist)

I was momentarily taken aback.

Did this mean I had to grow up?

Did it also mean she viewed me as somewhere between adult and child?

I didn't want to grow up, and I let her know. She explained that yes, I indeed would have to grow up, and once I did, I would be able to be a science. After unsuccessfully attempting to barter my way out of growing up, I told her that I don't believe you need to grow up to be a science, or anything else. I explained that the best science's I've ever met are kids.

Hailey had an almost visceral response to my words and was visibly horrified. "NO!" She exclaimed while shaking her head knowingly. "Kids can't be a science, Zo. You have to grow up, and then you can be something. We are just kids. We can't be a science."

We had uncovered a limiting belief. One where Hailey, at age four, had come to believe that to BE something, you have to grow up first. She had come to believe the absence of 'adulthood' equated to an inability to be someone. She had taken it on as fact, as just 'how it is.' In her mind, it was clear that you simply can't be something until you are big. Automation. Her belief was solid, unwavering, and automatically applied to all situations.

The limiting beliefs of a bygone era pose a significant threat to our children.

In our house, we have a saying, one we use when the word 'can't' comes into play.

Oh, there's a 'cant'...... just drop the 'T' and you can!

I threw it out into the wind. How would she respond? She paused for a moment, considered my words and then shook her head. "Kids aren't sciences Zo."

We left it at that, and I made a mental note to bring my awareness and, therefore hers, to a child's capacity for deep thought, powerful contemplation, and the thorough testing of theories.

For weeks I couldn't shake her words. "You HAVE to grow up, and THEN you can BE something." Where had this belief come from? How had it become so firmly, rigidly and unwaveringly cemented in her mind?

Then it hit me. I knew where she had gained it. And I was complicit!

"What do you want to be when you grow up?"

How many times did you hear that as a kid? It's a mainstay of general conversation, a throw-away phrase, and a conversation filler like "how are you."

What purpose does it serve? Why do we ask it? Do we ask it because we are genuinely interested in what the child in front of us is into, or are we asking it because it was asked of us so often as children that it's just a thing you do? There's a clue for somewhere to start as you uncover the beliefs you were gifted as a child. What are the things you do because its just a thing you do?

If we are truly interested in a child and their values, perhaps there are better ways to ask and if we are asking it because it's just a thing you do, can we just do away with it altogether because what ss the cost for our children when we are doing things because they are just a thing you do? By asking our kids what they want to be WHEN they grow up what are we robbing them of in their childhood?

By placing a future focus on BEING something, are we telling our children they aren't anything now? That they must wait? That when they are grown, they will magically morph into something? Into someone who IS someone?

Since the "You could be a science" conversation, I've been much more aware of my language. By bringing awareness to the language I choose, I have uncovered and dissolved a multitude of language faux pas. Everything from "Be careful" and "Good boy/girl" through to "Bless you" are out in our house alongside the age-old "What do you want to be when you grow up?"

We are programming our kids, regardless of parenting style, irrespective of the level of freedom and autonomy we afford them. We are programming them, always.

For this reason, I believe that just as we must speak of values with our kids, we must also speak explicitly, often and from early on, about beliefs. When we notice a firm belief in them or another, this is an opportunity to open a conversation, to bring it into focus. Let's look at a couple of examples of common beliefs.

You may hold a belief that products on the market in Australia must be good and safe to be there. Yet this is not always the case. We've got baby container syndrome as a result of cleverly marketed products that guarantee to contain and entertain infants so that adults can get back to it. These products do not serve our children or support optimal growth and development. And yet each year we see more and more products enter the market. Parenthood is a fabulous place to extend your research capabilities and approach each new season with curiosity and a desire to follow the latest research as opposed to the done thing.

Another commonly held belief is that babies haven't much to add to the conversation, unless you include crying. Babies simply aren't viewed as capable communicators. Our son Wahri has a lot to say, a capable communicator from birth. He figured out early that language and a firm finger point can clue the big people into what you'd like to take a closer look at. Shortly before his first birthday, we were running errands and having plenty of yarns along the way. Finding fans and wheels and all the things that go round and round alongside taking notice of all the different lights and needing to pause to inspect them.

As we were being served, Wahri pointed to the ceiling and loudly exclaimed, "L, Li." I responded, "light, yeah mate, there is a light." Wahri continued to stick his tongue right out while producing L sounds.

The young cashier promptly addressed me and told me "The baby isn't saying light. He's just a baby, and babies can't talk."

He wasn't right, but here's the thing. He also wasn't wrong.

He was basing his statement upon his experiences and how he filter's the world. In his mind, babies are not communicators. Belief right!

His filtering of the world in the 5 minutes before our brief interaction did not include him noticing Wahri pointing out three other lights, including a lamp and a salt lamp, nor was he aware that lights are one of Wahri's go-to things to notice and chat about.

I could have gone all in and educated said cashier on this particular babies capacity for communication. Instead, I simply smiled, looked back to my son, scanning the room for more lights, and asked, "Can you see any more lights?"

There may or may not be a cashier who thinks I've completely lost my mind. There is 100% a small person who knows I am listening. You know?

My point here is that what you believe influences your decisions, actions and subsequently, the language you use. It's not about swapping out the programming and beliefs of your childhood for another set from me, or anyone else. It's not about following my lead and adopting what I share with you in this book. It is my hope that this book will serve as a guidepost for you, that you come home to you and move forward with integrity in ways that feel right for you. I'd love to see you living squarely in your unwavering truth, unapologetically.

Adults unwavering and unapologetically living their truth, that's what our kids need to see, that's leadership.

CHAPTER FOUR

ATTUNEMENT

Attunement, it's those moments in family life when everything flows, when it's peaceful, and everything seems easy. It's easeful to be together. Your calm, your children are calm, there's harmony, and joy

In these moments, we can truly see our children in all their unique magnificence, and if we are open to it, we can also see the power and beauty of our mothering.

And yet, in other moments, family life isn't glorious. Joy and any sense of harmony seem to have been erased from your memory. You get caught up in the heaviness and run the stories of overwhelm and burnout.

It's always like this...

I never get to....

Why can't they just....

You hear me?

Be aware of the 'always and never' stories you tell yourself. When we experience these thoughts, it's easy to question our capacity, our sanity and search desperately for the elixir guaranteed to restore the flow!

It has been my experience that the difference between deep flow and connection, or NOT, is often my capacity for attunement.

The degree to which I have been aware, attentive and responsive to my own needs has a profound impact on my capacity for attunement.

If flow is the ocean, attunement is the skilled sailor.

And you know what they say about sailing?

A smooth sea never made a skilled sailor.

For the purposes of this book and your daily parenting practice, when I talk about attunement, I am talking about the art of emotionally sensing and joining with your child in a two person experience of connectedness. One where each person is acutely aware of the felt sense of the other and therefore tuned into and resonating with their experience, emotions and nervous system regulation of the other.

It's big. It's not something you can do or be all the time, that's the first lesson. It took me a while to recognise that aspiring for 100% attunement 100% of the time is a futile quest. One destined to end in disaster.

My journey with attunement began well before I had kids. From an early age, children flocked to me. People would often ask me.

How do you do it?

How do you engage with kids so effortlessly?

What are you doing differently?

Why do they listen to you?

I found these questions rather abstract. There's nothing special about me. I'm just doing what everyone would do. Aren't I?

There was something different about me. At that stage, I didn't know what it was. I couldn't reconcile it. How did kids in supermarkets, on the street, in parks or at the beach know I would listen attentively to and honour their experience. Aha, there it was.

Attentive honouring. But how did they know I was that person?

Children, unlike most adults, are highly intuitive beings capable of understanding the felt sense. Through this emotional sensing, children picked up on my capacity to be attentive to their experiences.

My involvement in the lives of children continues to shift as I navigate the experiences of my life, but one thing remains the same. I am fiercely protective of a child's rights and deeply passionate about freedom and autonomy for kids. Over time my passion grew, an attuned and intuitive child activist was born.

But I must tell you, the attunement required in the act of Motherhood has rocked me to my core. I've had days where I'm burnt out, exhausted and operating from a space of lack or scarcity. It has been my experience that when I am observing the experiences of my life through a lens of lack it is tough to cultivate and create space for deep and purposeful attunement.

In these moments, the training ground of Attunement, I choose not to focus on what I perceive I've lost. I choose instead to focus on shifting my perceptions around the situation.

Cultivating attunement requires a sense of abundance. It simply cannot thrive in scarcity.

Attunement may or may not come naturally to you. I recognise my experience is not the experience of many. This is an opportunity to pause and ponder, to get curious about your relationship with Attunement.

Are you fuelled by moments of deep connection, or do you run?

When you are deeply connected to your child, do you stay there, in the moment, or do you seek to 'get back to it?'

If you find yourself being drawn to getting back to it, this may be clear feedback that you are more comfortable in human-doing than human-being.

As you grow your capacity to BE, you'll benefit immensely, and so too will your kids.

Be here.

CHAPTER FIVE

CO-REGULATED AND CONNECTED

Your life is unique. You've lived a unique set of experiences, and these experiences have shaped who you are. Your capacity to maintain one foot in your own regulation while showing up to co-regulate your kids is governed by your brain architecture. You might find co-regulating your child easeful at times and absolutely, categorically impossible at others. There's nothing 'wrong' with you, there's no such thing as a perfect mother.

Your early life experiences literally lay the foundation for your adult brain. The way your earliest attachment figures soothed you and how their nervous system handled stress has wired your default program. How they dealt with nervous system activation can give you an indication of how you are likely to handle similar activation. If you, like me, have some trip wire triggers this chapter is an opportunity to disarm the charge and move forward.

Over the past 10 years, as I've come to understand the research, I find it astounding that our behaviourist approach continues to overshadow the critical importance of co-regulation in the early years. As a fully grown adult I still benefit immensely from the soothing calm and content energy of my husband.

Had a hard day? A hug from someone you love will help right? Co-regulation.

Feeling overwhelmed? You know just who to reach out to for a chat. Co-regulation.

Rageful and wild? Who is that one person you know who will witness you in that and whom can hold it without judgement, without trying to 'fix'? Co-regulation.

We are grown ass adults and we still need to be co-regulated sometimes.

Yet often our children are expected to hold it all together even when the adults are dysregulated. Why is it that children are held to a higher standard?

Picture this; everything is going smoothly and then out of nowhere, there's an outburst. Your child has gone from 0 – 100 at light speed, and you are left wondering what just happened.

You react...

"Calm down."

"It's not that bad."

"You're ok."

"Chin up."

"What's your problem?"

Hands up if one or more of these have passed your lips... Yeah me too. We've all reacted unconsciously instead of responding calmly and consciously.

Before I go any further, I just want to pause to recognise that we all make mistakes in this parenthood gig. When you realise you've fallen short, the most important thing to do is own it and make the necessary repair with your child. In doing so, you model the whole human-being experience. You'll model for them what you hope they'll draw upon when they are grown. Osmosis remember...

So, you've fallen short. You've said something to the effect of "calm down." Now what? We all know the chances of someone calming down by being told to calm down are about a million to one. This statement isn't helpful for me, and I suspect it isn't that helpful for you either. So why would we throw it out into the wind and expect it to work for children?

When we tell our kids to calm down, what we are really saying is that this thing you are displaying, it's too much. Too big, too loud, too inconveniently timed, and too much. Anger, rage, disappointment, sadness, fear, you name it, we see it and don't like it, so we tell it to go away. When we do this, we send a clear message to our children that it's not ok for them to feel the way they do. And so we tell them to push it down. Feel familiar? Often when we want or need that thing to go away, it's because we haven't the nervous system regulation to keep it together if we bear witness to it.

If we haven't the nervous system regulation to look at it and we want it gone, imagine how it feels to be the small person, the one navigating the situation, experiencing the emotions, and asking for help. Yes, help. Those behaviours we label as bad are simply communication. Once we can see them as such we begin to see situations in a whole new light. What we are doing here is creating the space for ourselves so that we can show up to help our kids when they need us, through co-regulation. Let's dive in.

To behave in socially acceptable and 'reasonable' ways, we must first have access to our prefrontal cortex. With brains built from the bottom up and from the inside out, this higher-order thinking part of the brain is one of the last parts to come online, I'm talking maturation in your mid 20's. Your prefrontal cortex is the decision-making part of your brain, responsible for your ability to plan and think about the consequences of your actions. It's the home of language, where your capacity to have empathy and impulse control resides. When your prefrontal cortex is offline, you cannot meet the demands of those around you, end of story.

Dan Siegel's hand model of the brain and the way he speaks about us 'flipping our lid' has been, in my experience, enlightening and life-changing. This book is all about bringing the unconscious into consciousness while looking at children and childhood through the lens of children coming to the world as whole and complete beings.

So, the prefrontal cortex is offline. What now? Imagine that you are your child. You are small and vulnerable, your prefrontal cortex is immature and any also offline in this moment. You are quite possibly misunderstood or labelled as 'bad' in your experience. It's a recipe for disaster. With the prefrontal cortex under construction through until our mid 20's is it any wonder our children fall short of being reasonable from time to time?

Toddler tantrums...

Terrible two's...

Threenager...

What you've got here is, as I see it, the most misunderstood and marginalised group of people on the planet. Almost all adults see the 'behaviour' of children in this age group as unacceptable, entitled, demanding and manipulative.

But when we understand how a human brain is built, how our brains were built in our early years of life, we can begin to see our young children through empathetic eyes. This sets us up to approach our children with care and compassion.

When we extend care, compassion, and reverence to our children, they develop the capacity to emulate that. Over time when we respond sensitively to our children's needs, they in turn, develop the skills and capacity for co-regulation that we would hope to see extended to us on our most unlovable days.

The bottom line, our children aren't doing the things they do to annoy us. They are doing the best they can. I'm reminded of this truth as I navigate the editing process for this book. It's mid-morning, and I'm thankful that our 11 month old son Wahri has fallen asleep in the car while running errands after an incredibly wakeful evening. It was the kind of night that saw me propped up on a mountain of pillows while breastfeeding, rocking, bouncing and humming to him while listening to my now least favourite soundtrack, on repeat, for hours!

I could have easily flipped my lid, lost control of my prefrontal cortex and thrown my hands in the air. But what would that have achieved? If rest was the desired outcome, those actions would be counterproductive to the cause.

As the hours passed and I continued to feed, rock, bounce and humm I wondered if I'd be still listening to this soundtrack as dawn broke. I was coming close to losing my cool. It was beginning to feel like he was absolutely doing this to me, that he was doing it on purpose. I could feel my energy rising, took a deep breath and smiled.

It wasn't that Wahri was doing this to me. Although my husband and I had been awake for hours us meeting his needs was nothing more than that, us meeting his needs! He was cutting teeth, and his immune system was mounting an attack on an unknown invader. He was congested, tired, hungry, and frustrated about trying to feed with a blocked-up nose. Have you ever tried to drink through a straw with a blocked nose?

He was as frustrated by the situation as we were, and he was simply asking us to show up, meet his needs, and share a bit of our nervous system regulation with him. To do any less would only exasperate the situation.

Yet wakeful evenings, and other intense mothering moments, haven't always played out like this. I've co-escalated situations almost identical to this in the middle of the night before. I've lost my cool, shouted to the universe that it's "All too hard" and walked off stomping. We won't get it right consistently. We won't be 'perfect' mothers. Instead, let us strive for present and purposeful over 'perfect' in our mothering. After all, present and purposeful feel free. Perfect feels like a cage.

I believe it is in our imperfection that we find our truth, our flow. By approaching ourselves with compassion in challenging times, we can set course for calmer waters. We develop the skills required to meet what we previously felt unable to. Skilled sailor, right?

Throughout my life, I've had an interesting relationship with regulation. I've witnessed and expressed the repressed transgenerational inheritance of anger and rage. Traversing transgenerational trauma, in my experience, is not conducive to feeling peaceful, calm, or well-regulated. As I write this chapter, I find myself deep in the trenches of uncovering and healing the deep hurts of my family lineage to end the cycle. It feels big, and that's because it is.

For much of my life, it's been my desire to support children to feel peaceful, calm and at ease. This desire, paired with my extensive experience navigating daily life alongside children, has given me the tools to support children through co-regulation.

As I cast my eye over my life, I can see that I've often used these same tools and strategies to regulate myself just enough to be able to co-regulate children, yet at other times, when there's no child around who needs to hook up to my calm nervous system, I can be pretty dysregulated. Introspection hey, it's a fascinating lifelong journey.

Although feeling calm and at ease isn't my default nervous system state, I feel immensely fortunate to have a lived experience that affirms my capacity to change the narrative, to break the cycle and forge a new way forward for our family. I now know that I can hone my skills while gifting my children the blueprint. This drives me as I uncover and heal the wounds of my family lineage.

Let me tell you about the arrival of our son, Wahri. His birth was a peaceful experience of deep connectedness. Wahri's birth was intense, transformative and calm. These aren't words I would choose to describe how I commonly feel. Feeling relaxed and at ease doesn't come easily to me. My nervous system simply isn't wired that way.

Wahri's arrival the crescendo in our journey through conscious conception, intuitive pregnancy and planned freebirth. Throughout this season of life, my husband and I devoured information. We read, researched, took courses, and bathed in natural, physiological, undisturbed birth energy. We put together a birth team to support our journey, but above all else, we came together in synergy to create an environment to welcome our child in ways that felt aligned and honouring for us.

Wahri entered the world through me, but his birth was where I found myself.

His birth was where I reconnected to me, the calm and content me.

I finally met me, as I was born to be.

You see, my body is usually on high alert. My default nervous system state is to scan, plan, and prepare for a myriad of circumstances that may or may not come to fruition. It protects me from feeling caught unaware, which supports me to maintain a functional level of regulation.

If you've already considered all the options and scenarios, you've just got to choose the best course of action when something occurs. It's a good strategy, until it's not.

Yet on the night of Wahri's birth, I was calm, at ease, free of the worry and what ifs that often plague my mind. I was deep in the practice of human-being.

Wahri's arrival was a truly transformative and monumental experience. Not only did we welcome our son, not only did his life's journey earthside begin, and not only did we birth him sovereign and free in our tiny home in the bush.

That night I also gained a point of reference for calm contentment well beyond any level of calm or contentment I had experienced. Ever!

I often draw upon this experience when regulation seems out of reach. I am able to access what feels different when I'm having trouble maintaining equilibrium. It's worth pausing to ponder the situations or circumstances that leave you feeling stretched or under-resourced. By doing this, you'll increase your capacity to co-regulate your kids.

Cultivating an environment that supports you to be calm, content, centred, and regulated is critical because we are always co-regulating or co-escalating our kids.

We aren't striving for perfection here remember. It's entirely possible that you'll fall hopelessly short at times. There are lessons here too. Use these as opportunities to model ownership while demonstrating repair after rupture.

Attuned observation paired with the awareness that I can either co-regulate or co-escalate in any given situation is, I've found, my greatest parenting asset.

What this looks like in practice for me is bringing my presence in, slowing down to notice that which would go unnoticed if I maintained my adult pace of doing and being and thinking and planning and pivoting and considering.

It's a pause.

It's breathing deeply, scanning my body, noticing if I am calm enough, regulated enough to co-regulate my child. I cannot co-regulate if I am not regulated. And neither can you. So, if I pause and realise I am not up for this right here right now I take that as feedback and set about creating an environment where we can all thrive. Regaining my capacity to co-regulate my children must be priority number one. What that looks like in practice is anything from the age old 'just add water' or shifting my expectations through to shifting the energy with an impromptu adventure.

Wahri was eight months old when I wrote this chapter, and I distinctly remember him having a morning nap on the bed next to me while I paused, pondered, and put pen to paper to share this with you. It was quiet, dark and peaceful. You know it's not always like that if you've got kids, especially with the altered sleep that developmental leaps and teething create. Let's just say we had experienced a few more of those 'wakeful' nights.

It was an uncharacteristic daytime nap on this particular day, one where my constant presence and body contact was not needed. I remember feeling myself exhale deeply as I experienced a brief reprieve from the intensity of mothering in this season. I had been gifted with an opportunity to anchor myself deeply in my own self-regulation and sense of calm so I could once again meet the intensity.

These moments, however brief they may be, allow for truths to drop in, be felt, and integrated. The embodiment of our mothering journey is paramount if we are to feel like we are doing this role, this immense and intense role justice.

I'm yet to meet a mother who does not want the very best for their child. We each take a different path, and we each see the world through different eyes. Although we may see the world differently and as a result our paths vary the desire to do the very best for our kids unites.

I've not met a parent yet that enjoys witnessing their child struggle. It is extremely difficult to bear witness to our child's pain, anger, frustration, hurt, and sadness, even more so when it 'sneaks up on us.' I anticipate you know this well. There's harmony in the home, everything is ticking along and then out of nowhere, or so it seems, a situation arises. In an instant, your full focus and attention are required.

If your child is ill or has hurt themselves, you spring into action at light speed. Nothing else matters. Your baby is hurt. That's your only focus. Right?

Why is it that can we find it challenging to meet our child with this same level of respect and reverence when it's not injury or illness?

When faced with the 100th outburst for the day, why can we tend to feel the energy rising in our body to the point of boiling over?

Co-regulating or co-escalating, remember!

What's it going to be?

It's your choice.

When I find it difficult to meet my child with reverence, I like to remember the river of integration, as Dr Dan Siegel puts it. Flow is the river. It's where harmony resides. From this place, we are well placed to meet our kids. The banks of the river are chaos and rigidity. When I'm finding it challenging to remain regulated so that I may co-regulate my child, I am on the banks, either in a state of rigidity or chaos. If my children bring me chaos in these moments, I meet them with rigidity. If they bring me rigidity, I meet them with chaos.

It's about me when I fail to keep one foot in my own regulation and join them in a dysregulated rigid state, what I NEED to get done. What THEY are preventing me from doing.

Similarly, when I meet them with chaos, I feel the need to get out of there. I can't handle it. I want to be anywhere except where I am. Get me out of here NOW!

If I fail to seek out ways to shift my energy neither scenario ends well, my capacity to effectively meet their needs diminishes and I don't parent in the way I desire.

When you fail to maintain nervous system regulation, your responses may look different to mine, or you may resonate with my experience. Regardless of what your experience looks like, it's essential to recognise your go-to unconscious patterning and programming so you can pause, ponder, and pivot. This is an opportunity to get curious about how you respond in moments of high intensity.

When your kids bring you chaos how do you respond?

When your kids bring you rigidity how does that play out?

When I am on shaky ground, I find it helpful to imagine my child saying, "Co-regulate me so I may learn to self-regulate Mummy!"

To demonstrate, let's look at an example. I recall a family afternoon down at the beach. We had pulled up for a swim, and Hailey, who was three at the time, was collecting shells along the edge of the tidal creek while we set up our camping chairs and snacks. Out of nowhere, or so it seemed to us, Hailey screamed and began flailing her arms and legs while in the shallows.

I ran to her, scooped her up in my arms and quickly checked over her body, looking for a visible sign of injury. The scream had been so sudden and loud that my first thought was injury. Had she cut her foot on a sharp rock? Upon realising there was no blood nor visible injury, I got out of my head and tuned into her.

She was going a million miles an hour. Her heart was racing, and I could hardly make out any of the words she was shrieking in my ears. I took a deep breath, pulled her body close to mine, looked her in the eye, calmly and slowly said, "That was a big fright. I was frightened you were hurt. I just ran over and scooped you right up out of the water. Are you ok?" Her eyes darted around, and she screamed hysterically.

I took another deep breath while trying to establish eye contact with her. I caught the words "hermit crab", so I asked, "Did you see a hermit crab?" "Yes, it touched me and...."

This is where she completely lost any language she had left and dissolved into a writhing, sobbing, squealing mess. Well, that's what it looked like to an onlooker. My husband and I exchanged glances that said, "Well didn't that go from 0 – 100 quick!"

You see, Hailey had encountered hermit crabs before. She had held them and observed them. She had helped her dad catch Mud Crabs in the rocks just up the beach earlier that very day. This didn't seem to make any sense. And to be honest, 'sense' was the least bit important in the moment.

This wasn't so much about the hermit crabs as it was about the autonomic nervous system response of fight, flight occurring in her body. Instead of trying to talk her through the situation, instead of running through her previous experiences trying to rationalise our way through it, I tuned into her body, looking for where she was holding tension. Looking for where was I holding tension. I was going to need to calm my nervous system after the sudden activation I'd experienced.

I sat on the sand with my feet in the water. I rocked with her and kept her feet up out of the water and 'harm's way.' I verbalised to her that I would keep her body up out of the water. I wiped the hair away from her face and washed the sand from her body. I held her close and kissed her forehead. I squeezed her arms and legs rhythmically. Deep pressure holds are an effective co-regulation strategy for Hailey.

I did all the things I've done so many times before to soothe her nervous system gently. Within a few minutes, her sobs had ceased, her smile had returned, and she told us the story of the surprise attack of the hermit crab. We laughed together, and she stopped mid-laugh to say to us "But it made me really scared, I didn't like it!"

We validated her feelings and expressed that we too did not enjoy unexpected frights. I took a mental note to help bring the unknown into the known when we next visited a beach that was likely to see surprise attacks. With Hailey, it is usually a surprise attack that derails her autonomic nervous system. And if I'm honest, it's the one that gets me the most.

This surprise attack signalled to her body that she was in danger. The stress hormone cortisol flooded her body and initiated the fight-flight response, a physiological response. It is important to remember that to the child, this is a big deal. This moment feels frightening, uncertain, unnerving and potentially very 'bad.' Remember, we've conditioned them to categorise things.

Instead of telling your child, "You're ok," or something to that effect, it is essential to show them safety. Through moving in slowly, calmly and with intention you can assist them through the gift that is co-regulation. Sometimes it is as simple as creating spaciousness, a cuddle, or a gentle hand. Spaciousness gives the body time for the stress response to dissipate, for the autonomic nervous system to calm and for them to FEEL ok in the situation.

As we touched on earlier, we cannot effectively co-regulate our children when we are in a dysregulated state. If your nervous system is activated and regulation seems out of reach, you may wonder how you can co-regulate your child. I get it. I too have felt this way. When faced with this situation, it's an opportunity to shift the energy.

Adjusting your day and the expectations you hold of yourself can be the remedy you need to get through. You might just find the intensity subsides. Drop the to-do list, swap out the elaborate meal you had planned for a quick go-to family favourite or something picked up on the way home. Essentially, shift the energy any way you know how.

The beach is my place. It's the place I'm most able to turn down the volume on the to-do list running around in my mind. When Wahri was an infant, we lived in a small beachside town a couple of hours from Darwin, Australia. We had long stretches of picturesque Northern Territory beaches to drive on only minutes from home. We now live on the Sunshine Coast and are spoilt for choice when it comes to beach adventures.

I've lost count of the number of times I've bundled the kids into the car for an impromptu trip to the beach. It's a place we can go to at a moment's notice. A bag with everything we need for a beach adventure packed and ready in the car alongside plenty of water for drinking and washing off sand.

By having this pre-prepared I can mobilise when I feel the energy rise. When I feel activated and unable to meet the intensity, we can be underway in minutes — shifting the energy, shifting the narrative, and creating a new way of being together in relationship, in family.

Without the beach ready bag, the overwhelm of trying to get all the things organised would likely see the family unit in a co-created cycle of co-escalation that would see me throwing my hands in the air and stating to the universe, "This is too hard!" Cue scarcity mindset and a perception of lack.

The core message here is this. You've got to be ok for the family unit to thrive. If you are moving about your day dysregulated, activated, and frazzled, that nervous system energy is going to flood through to everyone else.

Your children's capacity to develop self-regulation is governed by your capacity to model regulation and support them through consistent co-regulation. It isn't easy. It isn't something you can life hack your way through. It has been my experience that the way forward is through. If I am to emanate a co-regulated and connected energy, I must heal my wounds.

This parenting gig is a continual recommitment to heal our wounds, allowing our children to witness our growth alongside their own.

SECTION TWO

WISDOM YOU WERE BORN WITH

CHAPTER SIX

RITUALS

Ritual – A sequence of activities involving gestures, words, actions or objects.

When you were small, you understood ritual. You saw it all around. You likely understood it through the way you were soothed when you were frightened. You saw it in the way celebrations were prepared for. Ritual is everywhere, we are surrounded by it and immersed in it, yet we often fail to realise this is so.

Those things you do all the time, ritual.

Those things you do because someone said so, ritual.

Those quirky family traditions you only get if you are IN the family, ritual.

Yet not all ritual serves, nor does it need to continue. It's your choice.

What is the baggage of your family lineage dressed up in ritual?

Are there certain expectations, that to you do not make sense?

What are the things you do out of obligation, not alignment?

What would happen if you ceased to comply?

I believe that through the practice of parenting we called to seek out a life that feels nourishing, that is in alignment with our values. When you begin to shift your beliefs, you may find there are some rituals you are ready to let go of. You may just cease to comply.

Breaking cycles is not easy. It's ruthless, relentless and exhausting at times. But do you want what you got for your kids, or do you want something else? It's your choice.

Here's the thing, you will rub people up the wrong way no matter your choices. You will upset someone, somewhere along the line just by virtue of your very existence. It is better to have it as a result of living squarely in your truth than in service of someone else's ways. I love you. This is huge. What you are doing here is vast. And it's healing. You are healing the world, remember that!

What you do matters, what you do repeatedly matters more and what you value enough to create ritual around matters most. You are making memories here, core memories.

When your children are grown and have created the level of separateness that sees them moving in their own direction and creating their own family, those memories of ritual embedded when they were small will be all that's left of their childhood.

The more frivolous and fun the ritual, the more memorable to a child. Think silly songs or nicknames.

In short, rituals matter!

In our home, how we bring rituals into our day is a continual conversation. We find great value in asking ourselves what we believe to be true, what we value, and how that plays out through ritual. Our family rituals include...

Beach Sunday's

Where is your place? The place you go together to relax and unwind. In this place you each feel at ease, centred, connected, and calm. For us, it's the beach. For this reason, we've embedded beach Sunday into the flow of our week.

Our collective need for stillness and being in nature sees us putting beach Sunday into our schedule first and letting everything else fit in around it. We recognise that there is nothing more important than connection. If, for some reason, it cannot be a Sunday, we will create a pseudo-Sunday situation so we can have our beach Sunday on another day.

Connected Meals

A lot is going on in the relationship of family, multiple people all with their own priorities, values, and beliefs co-existing in a home. It's a place of extremes and intensity at times. For us, our mealtimes are an opportunity for a pattern interrupt.

We set the space with intent and honour togetherness. We all sit together and discuss our day. My husband Brendan and I recognise that we set the tone for the family through our energetic state, presence and attunement.

If we are scattered and rushed and thinking of all the competing priorities, it usually feels forced, disconnected. If what we seek is to honour togetherness then us arriving like this is counterproductive. For this reason connected meals are not a rigid, must be done each and every day at the same time thing. Similarly there are times where we recognise that our kids are not up for it and we honour this.

When we come together for connected meals we switch off the music, pack away toys and other distractions in the immediate area, and ensure there are no devices. We do not have a TV in our home, nor do we emphasise device use. As a result, we don't need to remove screen time from our mealtime rituals, but if you do have a TV and you too value the idea of connected mealtimes, this may be something you consider. Please take what resonates for you and leave the rest. This book is about reconnecting you to what You Already Knew alongside what you know to be true for your family.

Silly Rot

You know that weird and wacky stuff you do together as a family that sticks. The kind of thing you do once and from that day forward, your kid requires you to do it daily! Whether it be a silly rhyme created in the car to help you get the last five minutes to the driveway or a special handshake, the more ridiculous the better.

In my experience, all families have a certain level of silly rot. It brings fun and frivolity. It can quickly diffuse a tense or difficult moment. Silly rot is the kind of thing that people outside your immediate family unit either ask you to explain or find hilarious because they've never seen something so 'silly.' What's the silly rot of your life?

Phone calls between my husband and I often go something like this. "Harry!!. How are you doing Harry? What's going on Harry? Where are you Harry?" During the call, we are both Harry. Two Harry's having a yarn. I cannot even remember where or when it started, it's just a thing for us, and it consistently brings a smile. On particularly intense days, a cheerful "Harry!" coming down the phone is an invitation to breathe, get out of your head, and see a bit wider.

One five letter word, a pattern interrupt, an invitation to shift the energy. Magic! This is the magic of family, of relationship. Calls usually end with a "See you later

Harry, have a good afternoon Harry. We love you Harry, See you Harry, Bye Harry, Love you Harry!"

Connection Games

These little games are often unique to the family unit like silly rot. They serve to fast track a felt sense of being seen, heard and valued. Often, they are also special between two family members. They are micro-moments of connection that pack a punch. A way to get deeply connected quickly. Who doesn't need a little of that in their life?

Hailey and I have a connection game called "Goodnight little baby." To play goodnight little baby all that's required is me, her, my fabulously tragic singing voice, and an energy brought to the game to match hers. It is played directly after a shower or bath, and we've been at it since she was two and a half, early in our relationship together.

I remember bathing her, wrapping her in her towel and picking her up. It had been a big day for Hailey, full of swimming and beaching and adventure.

Her body was tired, but her mind was wired. I started swaying and singing to match her energy level but was singing the words "Goodnight little baby" repeatedly. The words didn't match the movements. She threw her body from side to side and giggled, yelling "more, more" and urging me to keep rocking hard and fast. I followed her lead and upped my game on the silly rot front.

Within a minute, her body softened, and she tuned into the words. Yawning and singing softly, "goodnight little baby." I slowed my rocking, drew her head to my shoulder, and whispered the tune into her ear. The bedtime situation looked a lot more like it would be a success. She went to bed, and I forgot about the silly rot connection song I had used to co-regulate her, until the next night.

As I wrapped her in her towel, she looked me in the eye and said, "Goodnight little baby?" Aha, noted small person, noted. As I tuned into her energetic state, I recognised that she was already calm. I met her where she was. There was no need for me to bring the previous night's level of intensity. As we swayed, Hailey led me to go slowly. I met her there. I varied my intensity, if I went up too high or down too low, she showed me where she wanted to be.

Each time she led me up or down, I verbalised what I was hearing from her body, and she squealed with delight when my spoken word confirmed for her that I was listening. We were playing with power now.

It has been my experience that playing with power and exploring ways to give your children the opportunity to feel powerful contributes to a sense of freedom and autonomy. Power need not be a dirty word. It's all energy. It's about giving our kids the opportunity to experience and express power in healthy ways.

Fast forward to Hailey at age six, and "goodnight little baby" remains a regular connection moment. We've modified and adapted the game as she's grown. One such modification I remember well was on her last night as an only child, where we sat quietly on the bathroom floor, rocking, and singing while I was in early labour. The dance itself is not so important anymore, it's the energetic exchange and nervous system synergy she craves, and if I'm honest, I too crave at the end of my day.

So, what does ritual look like in your family? And perhaps more importantly, where can ritual come into play in the intense moments to shift the energy?

CHAPTER SEVEN

I CAN DO IT

Our kids are capable from birth. Of that, I am certain. It's not the dominant narrative, not what we are sold. Yet it is true, and the evidence is all around if only we can see it. Knowing this truth and being able to honour it in the moment is an entirely different thing. So here I sit, metaphorically on my hands while focusing on regulating my nervous system. "He's capable" I remind myself. Why then, I wonder, is my jaw so tightly clenched? Breathe Zoe. He's got this. Tune into him, see the way he is focussing, see his competence, not the size of his body.

I'm watching Wahri mastering a new skill, and it's not my favourite, he's climbing higher than ever before, and he's given us the cue that he wants to do this alone. So here I sit, ready to pounce if he needs me. It's an interesting situation for me, I love to climb, and I've supported hundreds of children through this same milestone. Only this small person is my son, and he seems so tiny and vulnerable. And in some ways, he is. He's only 11 months old. But in so many other ways, he is so ready, his body is ready, and he's asking us to trust him. Up the slide and back down again is today's challenge. He's not yet walking consistently. He's not got a solid understanding of heights nor the amount of space his body occupies.

Yet he is determined that today is the day! Every fibre of his being is screaming, "I can do it", and who am I to say he can't? Drop the T, remember?

I know enough to know this is what he needs, but it doesn't make it easier. I've got an internal struggle on my hands. I'm reminded of Magda Gerber's words...

Do less,

Observe more,

Enjoy most.

I lean into my discomfort, allow it to be there and then shift my focus to him. He's got this. My husband is home, it's an opportunity for me to step back and allow him to be the one to spring into action if need be. His cat-like reflexes are quicker than mine, so I breathe easier.

I observe them with curiosity. They are calm, a shared determination in their eyes. My husband expertly follows Wahri's lead. He assists as little as necessary when invited and steps back when no longer required. His actions say.

I see you.

I trust you.

I am listening.

I believe in you.

I am here if you need me.

You are in control.

You can choose.

Choice's matter. Being trusted to make choices is essential, from birth. Think of a period of your life where you felt incredibly challenged, particularly misunderstood, and possibly even marginalised. How much choice did you have in that situation? Likely very little, it is entirely possible that a significant aspect of the challenge you experienced was as a result of feeling as if you had little or no choice in the matter.

The right to choose is a basic human need, as much as possible, as often as possible.

Yet this isn't often extended to children. "You can choose," we say, Bbut only within the bounds of what we decide."

Is it really choice if there is a list of approved options?

Is it really freedom if there are strings attached?

Is it really independence if someone is looking over your shoulder?

We've romanticised 'independence' in early childhood. We desperately want children to be independent. We want them to dress independently, put things away, calm themselves down, cope with change, play nicely and (if we are honest) quietly so we can DO the things. We chase it, push it upon children, and position ourselves as great parents because of how independent the world views our children.

We expect children to be independent and maintain control and equilibrium. As I see it, the problem is that we hold children to a standard beyond what we expect of adults.

Why is this?

Is it because this is how we were treated as children?

Or do we fail to see this inequality due to being so caught up in the adult realm?

It is incredibly difficult to see and understand the experience of a marginalised group unless you are a member of it. When I've paused to ponder these questions, and I've pondered them a lot, this is what I come up with.

As kids, most of us weren't trusted. We came to see ourselves as untrustworthy and began to seek answers from a higher authority. We were conditioned to look to the adults for what's true and correct. We carry on looking outside of ourselves into adulthood—always looking for the elixir guaranteed to gift us the answer to our questions.

The things we absorbed through osmosis when we were small have a profound impact on us throughout our lives. Therefore pausing, pondering, and pivoting is essential; you are changing the world through the cycles you choose to end. You are changing the trajectory of your children's lives and all the children after them by choosing a different path. You are an adventurer, a courageous explorer! Keep going!

I believe that if we could see through the eyes of our children, we'd make different decisions. Here are some common ways in which what we say and do are at odds.

We say be independent, then categorise and cage children by age.

We say be independent, then minimise and trivialise a child's innate wisdom.

We say be independent, then overlook children's creative genius.

We say be independent, then direct and dictate every aspect of children's lives to the point of complete exhaustion.

See the problem here? On the one hand, we say be independent, and on the other, we take away freedom and autonomy. We want independence, but we want it inside the confines, boundaries, and rules we set.

When I speak of children being caged, I am talking about how we categorise, sort and segregate children. I am not just talking about grouping kids by age in traditional schooling. It starts much earlier than that.

Looking for a playgroup? Let's find you one with kids the same age as yours. Going back to paid employment? Let me show you around the babies room. This is where all the children under two are grouped. They even have their own yard outside, a safe place separate from the older children.

And so, the segregation begins, children cooped up and caged, unable to move freely, unable to independently choose where and with whom they spend their time. It's as if we believe children to be incapable of making choices, but of course, that is precisely what we are saying, isn't it...?

On the one hand, we tell kids through our actions that they are incapable of being trusted while also requiring them to be capable of managing all their emotions and maintaining equilibrium from birth.

"Is he a good sleeper?"

"Does she cry much?"

If independence is what we truly desire, why do we find it difficult to give children the freedom to choose? I believe the answer lies in the perception of what it would mean if we were to hand the reins over to children. Afterall....

What would it mean for us if we viewed children as capable and simply supported their innate capacity to explore what is purposeful?

What would it mean for us if we stepped aside and invited children to create environments inspiring to them?

What would it mean for us if the children made the rules?

What would it mean for us if we children lived according to their natural rhythm?

What would it mean for us if we relinquished 'control' by allowing children to be in charge of what they explore?

Yes what would it mean for us if the children led the way?

To lead is to be heard, yeah? You've got to be heard, valued, and respected to take the lead and have others follow. How powerful is that? Now imagine you are a young child and the big people have extended that level of reverence for you. Yet this is often not the case for kids. It's not uncommon for children to feel unheard, undervalued, untrustworthy, invisible even. This is a story about a tiny person's experience of leading the way through being heard, witnessed, and understood.

The day is new, the birds are enjoying the warm sunshine, and we've just gotten up. I'm making a cup of tea. Wahri is moving about the house exploring and playing and chatting to himself. He's recently turned one, and I hear him coming towards me up the hallway. "Tom Tom, Tom Tom Tom," he says as he approaches.

I run the mental map of our house and consider the options of where his beloved Tom Tom (Thomas the tank engine) is. I continue making my cup of tea and am poised and ready with the top three options of where he might find said Tom Tom. He gets to the kitchen and again says. "Tom Tom, Tom Tom." I repeat "Tom Tom" back to him and start to tell him where Tom Tom may be.

He stops dead in his tracks and takes a deep breath. This is where I clue on. I've made an incorrect assumption here. I turn to look at him. He locks eyes with me, makes an obvious hand gesture and says, "come!" Aha, here's a new word. "Oh, you want to go somewhere?" I ask. "Where are we going mate? You lead, and I'll follow," He leads me to the garage. "Door door," he says. "You want to go through the door?" I ask.

He places his hand on the door and pushes, signaling yes. I open the garage door. He walks quickly through it and across to the roller door. "Door door." He says. Without asking him to confirm what he's already told me, I open the roller door. He walks out the door, turns to look at me, and gestures for me to come. He follows the gesture up with "walk" and casually wanders off. Just like that, our morning has pivoted. We're going for a walk up the street in our pyjamas, and my tea is going cold on the counter.

For our children to know that their voice matters when they are big, they must come to understand that their voice matters when they are small. If we are to raise children who speak up and stand up, we must raise them knowing they are heard and valued now. Wahri made it abundantly clear that he wanted to go for a walk, and there was no reason we couldn't, so I chose to follow his lead. I want my kids to grow up connected to their desires and with a deep knowing that their desires are purposeful.

In your parenting practice and daily life, I invite you to follow your kid's lead often. In the relationship of family, there's space for everyone's needs to be met. Changing the narrative from praise and punishment, instruction and compliance also sees us looking at how we distribute power and leadership in the home. It's a shift from the 'you get what you get, and you don't get upset' paradigm. After all, agency and the autonomy to lead are the foundational building blocks of independence.

I believe children would sum it up for us in this way. They'd say –

"We will become independent adults relative to the trust you placed in us when we were small."

Yet the quest for independence in childhood asks us to go further. To see wider. It asks us to extend the same freedom we experience to our children. It asks us to cultivate a nurturing environment that supports freedom and autonomy for all.

As adults, we have a lot of freedom to choose. Even when we feel like our freedom or right to choose is being threatened, we have a lot of freedom throughout our day—much more than is commonly extended to children.

Our children are over-scheduled and overwhelmed. There's little room for slow days, spaciousness, and freedom to explore. Our kids are starving for choices, for the opportunity to lead the way in their day. Is it any wonder we see what is commonly labelled as 'behavioural issues?'

I don't know about you, but if someone managed my schedule and kept me running day in day out, I'd probably have a few 'behavioural issues.' What if all it took was for us to extend the daily freedom and autonomy we experience as adults to our children, to the world's children?

I'm yet to meet an adult who loves to be told what to do, when and how to do it. Imagine your reaction if this were to occur. Imagine I come into your home while you're washing the dishes. It's a task you've done more times than you'd care to count. You need no instruction from me, yet I take it upon myself to do just that.

I tell you that you are doing it wrong. I tell you to use the dishwashing liquid I use and demand that you do it the way I say from this point forward. I top it off with a "because I said so" when I see you go to respond.

How would you feel? Now imagine I begin barking my next order at you before you've had a chance to reconcile what just happened. I tell you to stop washing the dishes because I need you to come with me, immediately. I turn my back and walk away. Only I stop a few paces away, spin around and glare at you as if to say, hurry up, I said now!

Feel familiar? It is entirely possible that you found yourself in situations not dissimilar to this as a child. Can you remember?

If this situation was real and happened to you today, how would you respond?

Would you comply?

Would you protest?

Or would you hold silent resentment towards me under the conditioning of a forced smile and obligatory compliance?

It's a ridiculous scenario. Yet kids often experience scenarios like this. Is it any wonder they've become adept at evasive measures? Is it any wonder they've cultivated a capacity for wilful ignorance and downright 'defiance?'

Upon closer inspection, these seem like creative, if not complete genius strategies to avoid the frustration and discontent of such disrespectful situations. Are we stripping away the freedom and autonomy of childhood under the guise of good parenting?

But where is the line between extending freedom and autonomy to our kids and being held hostage to their timeline? Fantastic question. I'll give you an example of getting everyone's needs met.

You've got yourself a wrestling, screaming, kicking, thrashing writhing toddler. For the purposes of this example, let's imagine you are at the beach and trying to leave. It's been an enjoyable outing, with plenty of free play and exploration opportunities. You sense that this is your opportunity to pack up and go. There's been much fun and laughter, but now you are trying to wrap things up. You gather your gear and say, "Let's go." This is where it gets salty, the limbic Olympics is what comes next.

You feel yourself becoming frustrated and activated. It's hot, the sun is beating down, and you can feel that everyone is a short few minutes from realising they are starving. If you are going to get out of here without a complete family meltdown, it has to be now.

Only your child won't go. They dig their heels in, become an immovable object, and scream "NO" at you.

Here's the thing, their NO isn't really at you, and it's not about leaving. Your child's firm "NO" is quite likely their best attempt to express to you that they are not ready for this to be over. Your casual "let's go" is quite likely the first they've heard of this experience coming to an end. They haven't been checking the clock in order to make a calculated decision about when to go.

They've been here, in the moment, enjoying life. Did you notice?

Now I realise none of this helps you resolve your very real need to go. How do we proceed in a way that gets everybody's needs met? You could become rigid and tell them that this is happening, and the message your child would receive is that what you say goes. Sound familiar? Or you can choose to see this as an opportunity to lean in, to see the situation from your child's perspective.

Ok, there's a kicking, screaming, writhing toddler in front of you. What next? The first thing you are going to want to do here is connect. Draw upon your knowledge of your child, how do they like to feel connected? Here's some ideas that might work.

Get down on their level with open body language.

Catch their eye with yours if you can, even if only momentarily.

Emanate pure love and understanding in their direction.

Remain open. If you close, they'll close.

Breathe. Manage your nervous system.

Be there, with them.

Feel what it would be like if you didn't have to go. You'd like that too.

Allow them the space to feel and express how their emotions. When they do, bring language to what you see.

"You don't want to leave, and that feels unfair. Imagine if we could stay all day long, even after the sun goes down!"

Once you've connected, you'll be well equipped to redirect them and leave the beach. It may take a little longer than simply announcing "let's go" and requiring immediate compliance, but you'll show your child that their voice matters.

Extending freedom and autonomy to children looks like;

Extended periods of uninterrupted play.

Living free of judgement and adult agendas.

Freedom to make decisions in matters that affect them.

Respect and reverence for what kids are doing, like actually doing, not what we think they are doing.

When you extend freedom and autonomy to your child, you'll inevitably leave the house with a toddler loudly and proudly rocking a mismatched outfit. It'll look ridiculous in your eyes but hey, their body their choice!

You'll be late to the thing due to respecting your child's decision to wear their new lace-up shoes that they simply must conquer tying on their own today.

Things will inevitably take longer and look differently than you had imagined, and this is precisely the point. If things are going along as planned it's a pretty clear indicator that there's only one person making decisions in family inc, and it certainly isn't the children. By relinquishing your need for control you'll be able to delight in the creative spirit of your child as you witness them gain the skills necessary to become the independent adult you desire for them to be.

CHAPTER EIGHT

WORDS MATTER

I've always known that words matter, it's a core truth for me. The words you choose can quite literally make people feel small and insignificant or inspire and encourage. That's powerful stuff. I'm wary of people whose language tends to demand compliance at all costs.

The way you choose your words and the emphasis you place on those words matters. Often when we are feeling all high vibe, positive energy and revitalised, it's much easier to choose words that inspire and encourage.

It's not only spoken words though. It's what we think about and say to ourselves too. You could call this the story of our life, the story we tell ourselves anyway. I ask you, what is the story of your life?

When we feel disconnected, it has been my experience that the capacity to communicate clearly and with intent suffers. The further I drift from calm contentment, the less my words inspire or encourage.

Have you noticed that the more stressed you are, the harder it is to communicate clearly? We tend to stumble over our words and get short and sharp, abrasive even! When I find myself here, in the space of unmet needs, resentment and little language to accurately ask for what I need, it usually results in the situation being exacerbated. And the worst part, it's me who exacerbated the situation.

I have got a lot to say, and for the most part, I can communicate my thoughts, feelings, and opinions clearly to those around me, until I can't. Because sometimes words are hard. When that prefrontal context is offline, words are so hard. Except for the four letter swear words, I've still got those! When words flow, it's much easier to choose then consciously. It's in the moments of chaos or rigidity where the words can become a problem.

We've all got a set of words that we live by. What are your words? The ones other people pick up from you. The common threads in your conversations? You might find they align with your values and beliefs. If the words you live by aren't immediately apparent to you, it's ok.

Get curious about the words you choose and the words of others. It may even be easier to start there.

Think of someone you love dearly.

What words or phrases come to mind when you think of them?

What are the words of their life? The words they live by.

Now think of someone you'd rather not have the unfortunate 'pleasure' of being in the presence of.

What are the words of their life?

How have those words or phrases impacted you?

What I've noticed is that we are more likely to downplay nasty or hurtful words when they are directed at children. Comments and statements like "oh that's just the way she is" are commonplace. It is as if we are more willing to side with an adult than to risk their disappointment as a result of us holding them to account for the words thrown out at children.

Why is this? Is it that we don't want to cause a scene? Is it that we believe that to respect one's elders is to remain silent even if those elders are out of line? I was gifted the opportunity to delve into my beliefs, values, and conditioning on this while writing this book. While visiting the local shopping centre to pick up some groceries and supplies we encountered a nasty woman. She very nearly ran our 14 month old son down with her cart and hurled vile words spoken with vicious intent in his direction.

In the moment, I was completely taken aback. I had no words. Not like me at all. Truth be told, I fear that had I spoken in the moment, I would have acted in ways I'm not proud of. And so, I stayed silent. Dancing between my fight, flight, and freeze response options. Unsure if I would stand and fight, run and hide or drop to the floor.

An open letter to the woman in the shopping centre.

You had the pleasure of occupying space with my son recently. Yet you didn't see it that way.

Instead, you were nasty. Your words bitter and your presence frightful. You made a little boy cry, do you know?

There's a train by the shopping centre entrance, have you noticed it? Wahri has.

That's my son's name, the little boy you verbally abused. Perhaps you'd care to know.

Wahri, at age 14 months, is fascinated by trains. His face lights up each time we arrive at these particular shops, for he knows he will soon see his beloved 'Tom Tom.'

On the day you crossed paths with us my son was making his pilgrimage to 'Tom Tom.' Set down on the floor from afar to make the journey under his own steam. Only the journey wasn't to play out the way it usually does.

You see, you changed all that. You entered his sphere of influence by occupying the same space and altered the course for a small boy joyous and free making his way to 'Tom Tom.'

Did you see his joy? No, I think not.

Instead, you set your course, an immovable object.

Instead, you set your jaw. A scowl intent on sending a message.

Instead, you set upon a child. Words thrown out at him like hot lava.

Are you proud of yourself for terrorising someone so small?

Do you feel powerful as a result of exerting power in his direction?

When I look at you, I do not see pride nor power. I see a nasty woman.

When I witnessed you make a slight course correction towards Wahri with your cart, I was taken aback. Surely, I was seeing things?

When I heard your vile and nasty tone bark, "get out of my way, or I'll run you over", I lost my breath. Surely, I was hearing things?

When I watched you walk away while I scooped my son up from the ground, I wondered what had led you to be so bitter.

As I sit here and pen this letter to you, I've some things to say. I was raised in a time where "if you haven't got something nice to say don't say anything at all" reigned supreme.

Upon witnessing your actions, I had no words to say, I couldn't believe my eyes.

Today I must stand up and say something. The way you treated my son was not acceptable. Setting out to terrify small children is not acceptable.

You may say, "he's got to respect his elders."

I say, we will instil in our son that respect is earned, not automatic because of age. Your actions were rude, nasty, and disrespectful. You are the first person to whom our son has a reference point for what nasty is. Do you feel proud?

I'm sorry if when you were small, no one saw the magic in you.

I'm sorry if treating small people like you treated my son has been normalised to you.

I'm sorry if you have not been treated with kindness, and as a result, you are ill-equipped to extend kindness to others.

I'm sorry if you were having a particularly hard day and felt like exerting power would make it better.

I'm sorry if you feel this is how children ought to be treated. I am here to tell you it is not.

You see, I understand the critical importance of early life experiences. I understand intricately that how we treat kids leads to how they are as an adult.

Child-rearing practices must progress as we come to understand more. The evidence is clear. Gentle, responsive, engaged, and attuned adults and approaches to parenting are the way forward. For those who know better, do better.

If we are to raise children to be whole and complete adults, we must change how we view children and childhood. No longer will "because it's always been done that way" cut it.

You were a nasty woman indeed on the day we crossed paths. Today, I hope you can see that there is another way. Today, and every day that follows I hope you see the magic in children around you.

Yours sincerely,

Zoe Haack

Child Activist

It is likely that you too, have encountered situations like this one and it is entirely possible that you also walked away a little dazed and confused. Knowing what to do when presented with such situations is really tough. How do we stand up for our kids while also modelling for them appropriate behaviour?

I believe that our power lies in our capacity to simultaneously hold people accountable for their actions while advocating for our children's rights. That's why I wrote this open letter and included it here for you. I hadn't the words in the moment, but I have them now. I will be equipped to hold people accountable while advocating for my kids if we face similar situations in the future. I won't tell my kids to stay silent if they haven't anything 'nice' to say. To do so does them a disservice and perpetuates a cycle of big people being let off the hook for abhorrent behaviour.

Saying what you mean and meaning what you say extends beyond the spoken word, but of course, You Already Knew that. In pondering the words that you choose to use, it can be helpful to develop some scripts or alternatives. We've already explored several of them in this book.

Be careful

You're ok

Good boy/girl

Hurry up

Come on, quickly!

Because I said so

That's enough

Don't cry

The way you choose your words and the emphasis you place on words matters. What will be the words you are remembered for? And perhaps even more importantly, what will be the words that you omit?

CHAPTER NINE

OSMOSIS

To heal the world is to raise children who will create a world unrecognisable to us.

If we are to succeed, the world our kids will create will be beyond recognition. This can only happen if we rethink, repattern and reorient what we think we know about 'teaching and learning.'

We are seeking to raise a generation of kids to do a better job with the planet than we have done and how they will do that is beyond the bounds of what we can recognise, of what we can reconcile in our minds. We must change the way we do things if we are to raise free thinkers who have the capacity and courage to create change that changes the course of humanity.

Now you may be wondering how on earth we do such a thing, how can we instil in our kids the kinds of lessons that will see them succeed at such a mammoth task. The answer may surprise you. We don't have to do anything, well not really. Instead, we must step aside, hand over the reins, and let our kids become who they were born to be.

Kids are inherently free thinking philosophers capable of potent pondering. Success lies in the questions, not the answers and therefore, our children's ability to create a world unrecognisable to us lies in our capacity to trust them to ask the big questions.

We know that there is an immense orchestra at play during childhood. Brains are being built in front of our very eyes. Our kids are naturally primed to seek the stimulation needed in the complex orchestras we call child development and maturation.

Let's take walking as the example. In the absence of illness, injury, or disability, no one needs to 'do' anything for children to acquire that skill. Little by little, day by day, we stack the experiences of our lives on top of each other until we master the next new thing. Learning to walk for most is no big deal. There are the inevitable falls and setbacks along the way, but it is otherwise unremarkable. Of course, it isn't viewed that way. It's seen as this significant, colossal achievement worthy of being commented upon by all who bear witness. I often wonder what our world would be like if we approached some of the less visible growth and skill acquisition with as much focus as that of walking.

In every moment of every day, we have the capacity for growth. It's been there since conception. No one had to educate your mother on how to grow you in utero. There is an immense orchestra at play that starts strong and often becomes silenced or overpowered by what we call 'teaching' and 'learning.' Here's the thing, there's so much that You Already Knew. There's so much your child knows.

Children know connection.

Children choose love.

Children seek to understand.

Children are philosophers, from birth.

Our kids are creating a map of themselves, and how they relate to the world, in their minds based upon what we tell them is important. If we focus too heavily on 'teaching' and 'learning', we rob our kids of the opportunity to follow their own path. Their map becomes filled with 'should' superhighways, and the side tracks and hidden gems fade away. Let me put it to you another way. I call this "shhhhh, be quiet."

You are an infant, the adults are tired of your crying. "Shhhhh, go to sleep." A good baby is a quiet baby.

You are two and have discovered a new noise. "Shhhhh, stop making that noise, you are too loud!" Loud = bad.

You are four, nasty words were spoken to you and hurt your heart. You cry. "Stop crying, you aren't a baby." Only babies cry.

You are six and raise your hand on the mat. "Let someone else have a turn." You lower your hand and gaze. Ideas don't matter, turns do.

You are eight and you've mastered something you've been focussed on for ages. You share your excitement and enthusiasm with those around you, but they say you are bragging. Nobody likes a bragger.

You are 10 now and you've got a lot worked out. You see something that's not right, so you stand up for yourself. They say you are overreacting. Strong opinions are not wanted here.

You are 14 and find yourself between worlds. You aren't a child yet nor are you an adult. The adults want you to "grow up." You don't like the look of what they want you to grow up into.

You are 16 and in hot water. The adults are mad. "You have to take things seriously." Fun is out of bounds now.

You are 19, a lot has changed since you were told to "shhhh" when you cried as an infant. The world seems unfamiliar, and you are unsure of your place. "Do something with your life" they say. You wonder what it is they think you've been 'doing' for the past 19 years if not living life...

You are 30 and gazing at your newborn. You are at a crossroads. Do you rinse and repeat or rewrite the map?

I want my kids to have maps filled with sidetracks, gems, and picturesque places off the beaten track. Places they've discovered, places they cherish and places that lead them home.

So here is the thing, If I want that for my kids, I've got to be willing to go and get it for myself. I've got to pull out my map, look at the well-worn paths, and ask myself if these serve. Do they take me where I want to go? My map may look a little like yours. Be a good mum, don't complain, keep on top of everything and be happy. There's little room for creativity on these roads. There's little room for freedom either. And so, I dance with the chaos and rigidity of my map of origin and my map of freedom.

What's your map of origin?

What did you learn through osmosis when you were small?

How does your map of freedom differ?

I believe we can shift the way we think about teaching and learning within a generation if we focus less on what kids can learn from us and instead focus on growth through osmosis. We know our kids are absorbing and taking in new information through osmosis. The question is, what are they absorbing?

You might wonder how focussing on growth through osmosis differs from teaching and learning. Learning is defined as 'the acquisition of knowledge or skills through study, experience, or being taught.' Somewhere along the lines, the emphasis has been placed on being taught, and to be taught, you must have a teacher, right?

It puts the power in the hands of those who 'know' the subject matter. It places the child into the passive role of receiving information, knowledge, data, the lesson. There's no space for pondering the big questions, theorising, and exploring from a philosophical standpoint in explicit teaching and learning. Our role, as the one being taught, is to receive that which is being taught. There's little room for philosophy in traditional classrooms.

We have created systems and checklists and tests and scores to measure the success of education while leaving growth, expansion, creativity, and individuality behind. I believe our kids have been dealt a great disservice in doing so.

How did we come to be here?

With the focus geared towards being taught, it's easy to forget the value of acquiring knowledge through experience.

How have we come to see learning as synonymous with being 'taught?'

Why is growth through osmosis so undervalued?

Let me introduce you to an idea. You may have even pondered this yourself. I believe it all comes back to trust. If children are not to be trusted, a commonly held view, why would we trust them with their learning?

Why would we provide them with the space and resources to direct their learning? Why would we value intrinsic motivation to support the acquisition of knowledge and skills?

We wouldn't....

And so, as a society, we don't.

See the problem?

But what if we did?

What would the world be different?

I'm here to tell you that you can change the narrative in a world where children are rarely consulted, largely silenced, and viewed as incomplete. Through your parenting, you can create the shift. You can be the adult the world's children can rely upon to trust them. You are a visionary if you trust in, consult with, and see children as infinitely capable. To see children this way is to recognise a child's capacity for immense growth, as if by osmosis. The question is...

Can you see it?

If you are reading this book, I have a feeling you can. You likely believe children are innately wise and complete.

What do you do with that information once you've seen what cannot be unseen? What does it mean for the way you engage with our world's most precious resource, children?

Well, it's simple, you commit to relinquishing control—hand over the reins. If the children of the world could tell us one thing about 'learning', this is what I believe they would say....

Our horizons expand through exploration. Step back, let us lead, step back and let us play.

Kids need breadth, not depth—the opportunity to explore far and wide. To try new things, explore unchartered territory and follow their heart. This may look like chaos to you.

It looks like things spread out across the floor.

It looks like pillow forts that require every sheet and blanket to come out of your linen cupboard. You hadn't realised that the contents of your linen cupboard were quite so mismatched until this day.

Children flit from one interest to another only to return to the earlier thing that initially caught their eye. There's purpose here too. Your child is being led by desire, led by what feels good. Can you remember?

Think back to your childhood. Can you remember what you found deeply purposeful? How much freedom did you have to explore that? Who were the adults who supported you to explore? Was play, especially the messy kind, valued in your home? How do the experiences of your childhood influence parenting decisions when your child finds a new interest?

Let's look at a couple of examples of how your family of origin and upbringing could play out in your parenting. If sticking to your word and following through at all costs was a core value in your home, you may believe that if your child doesn't follow through with something, they will be incapable of following anything through as an adult.

If changing your mind about what you are interested in was met with a dismissive tone or comments like "you change your mind more often than your undies," then perhaps you find yourself rolling your eyes when your child voices their latest discovery or interest. How much is this one going to cost you?

Resist these unconscious automatic family of origin responses and instead look deeper. Look to your child with curiosity and seek to see below the surface. What are they communicating to you through their new interest? Here's an example.

As I write this book for you Hailey is right into gymnastics. In the grand scheme of things, she hasn't a solid understanding of what competition gymnastics will require. But she is all in on loving it sick. Only she's an ankle injury, and it's coinciding with her offer to step into competition gymnastics. The knowledge that she cannot practice her craft right now hurts her more than the ankle injury. And here's why, she's created an identity for herself as a gymnast, and at age six, she's placed a lot of her worth in her ability to do handstands and the splits.

Suppose, as parents, we chose to place all our focus on healing her ankle and fail to see how important her proclaimed identity as a gymnast is to her in this season of her life. In that case, we run the genuine risk of having her feel disconnected, misunderstood and completely alone.

We must look to her and find ways to let her lead, even in a state of injury. What that looks like for us right now is creating space and opportunities for Hailey to immerse herself in the energy of gymnastics. She is researching gymnastics, watching gymnastics routines, devouring information about how the foods we eat fuel our bodies, talking about gymnastics and exploring it in every way possible. At the same time, she gets around in a moon boot.

She's still feeling the sting, and her feelings are welcomed and worked through in ways that feel good for her. If we approached growth through the traditional 'teaching and learning' paradigm, we would look for ways to distract and refocus Hailey's energy elsewhere. Instead, we lean in and let her lead where she can, however possible. What ensues is the kind of growth through osmosis that makes the heart sing.

A child exploring multiple ways to remain connected to her craft, acquiring skills and knowledge in any way she knows how. When her ankle is healed, when she is finally able to return to gymnastics, she will do so with a newfound understanding of the nuance of gymnastics paired with knowledge about the fragility and simultaneous strength of our bodies.

Or she may not. There's every chance that she may choose to go in a completely different direction. She may wake up one day, decide her quest to understand gymnastics is complete, and move on to something else. And if that is the case, she will have gained what she needed to, and we will honour her in her felt sense that this chapter is complete.

We must resist the urge to control our children's interests. We must resist the desire to ensure they are consistent at all costs. These are adult burdens, adult questions, and adult concepts to navigate. We need not burden our kids with the 'what if's' that plague our minds. To do so would only take away the pure joy of childhood.

I'm not saying you must rush out and buy everything they desire on a whim. It doesn't mean you have to enrol them in those ballet classes because they've discovered dancing this week.

When our kids bring new interests, they want us to know about them. They want to share their discovery and hear us delight in them. In these moments it's less about what we do and more about how we make them feel. So, reflect their joy back to them through your smile and actions.

You'll know before long if this is an exploration aligned with your child's values or not. It'll either hang around as Elsa has around here or taper off as ballet classes did for me as a kid.

You may also find that you tend to get behind the interests your children bring you that affirm your values. It's the ones that challenge our values or beliefs that can be difficult to traverse.

When I think back to my childhood, I remember the music. The music my mother chose communicated how she was feeling. This insight into her mind was profound. As adults, my siblings and I each have a playlist of our mother's favourite music in our minds.

Music was an integral aspect of my childhood, yet I wouldn't describe anyone in my family as particularly musical. None of us have written, played, or created music. I did hassle my Mum for an electric guitar as a teenager. I got one. I hadn't a clue how to use it nor a mentor to sit with me while I fumbled around orienting myself to the language of music and, as a result, gave up on becoming a musician quickly.

My husband plays the guitar, and he does so with an 'it's no big deal' attitude. He's self taught, as with many of his varied skills. His curious nature and intuition take him in many different directions. Breadth! His guitar playing is this astounding skill I'm not sure I have the patience for.

However, simply by bathing in the energy of his music, by observing him and being present in that experience, I am beginning to understand basic concepts of how to play the guitar. I am acquiring knowledge, through osmosis.

Our son Wahri bathes in his Daddy's music almost daily. It's something he craves. If he sees Daddy's guitar, he 100% must have Brendan play it. I can see the immense beauty in how these day to day experiences form part of Wahri's relationship with his Dad and the very fabric of his childhood.

By focussing on bringing breadth to our parenting we get to expand as our kids do.

Got something you've wanted to explore for ages but haven't? Now's your chance.

See your child seeking knowledge on something you don't have a clue about? Why not explore it together.

When we focus less on 'teaching and learning' and instead emphasise expansion and growth through osmosis, we are free to explore. So go forth and explore with your kids. Gain new skills, try your hand at the new hobby, not because you'll be good at it but because you'd like to have a go!

Look for people in your network who are knowledgeable, skilful, and passionate in these areas. Invite them to share their passion with you and your child.

We see infinitely more value in our friends and family sharing their passions and knowledge with our children over a present purchased at a shop. It is for this reason that we emphasise presence over presents. When people speak of their passions, the conversation is enthralling. Let's raise enthralling kids!

Here's the thing, when we commit to handing over the reins to our kids, we've got to be solid in our sense of freedom and power. I know that if I am feeling out of control or powerless, my parenting shifts into one tainted by my desire to regain that which I perceive has been lost, freedom.

The other thing I know to be true is that regardless of your worldview on teaching and learning, there will be times when it will feel like progress is painfully slow. You may even feel like you are going backwards, regressing. Things that were in flow a few days or weeks ago come to a crashing halt, and everything needs to be rejigged, AGAIN! You'll wonder what went wrong. You'll seek to find what or who is to blame and set about putting something in place to solve said problem. Enter rigidity. Rules and requirements and non-negotiables that don't quite make sense.

But if you can find the capacity to pause and sit in the discomfort, you might find it's not a setback. You are simply between who you were and who you are becoming. Or, more specifically, who your child was and who they are becoming.

**If you can stop for long enough,
you'll see it's not coming apart.
It's coming together.**

If you can find the capacity to pause, a day will come where all the minor incremental shifts, changes and growth come together. When this happens you'll catch yourself looking at your child with greater reverence. You might even gain a renewed sense of wonder for the immense orchestra of growth in your child's mind, body, and soul every day!

These days, in the relationship of family, you are reminded that you are living, breathing, and experiencing life together during the most incredibly crucial period of your child's life. As parents, we are the stewards of our children's childhood years. Capable of providing them with a breadth of experiences and opportunities that serve to broaden their horizons, their understandings and their capacity to see the world through eyes wide open.

CHAPTER TEN

PLAY IS PURPOSEFUL.

Welcome to the play chapter. You've arrived at the place from which a great rediscovery occurs. Are you ready to regain your playful nature?

When you think of play, how do you feel? Does the word play bring up feelings of excitement, joy and wonder for you, or does it inspire a sense of chaos, noise, and mess? If it's the latter, let's look for ways to increase the joy of play, playing and playfulness for you.

We've explored cultivating a connection to self, reconnecting to intuition and we've prioritised observing our parenting with curiosity and compassion. We've looked at how play has been demonised or given significance by calling it a child's work, but we haven't yet delved deeply into the role of play. This chapter is about celebrating play and, in doing so, celebrating our kids.

Just

As

They

Are

If a child is given the opportunity, they will play. Through play, the child gains everything needed in just the right dose, in just the right order, with just the right expectations.

Play is what children do, always.
End of story.

Before I go any further, I must preface that play, the true authentic kind requires the absence of adult agendas, the absence of interruption and the absence of structured 'learning.'

I'm often asked to speak on the concepts of work and play, and I make it my mission to send one message loud and clear.

No, I do not believe play is a child's 'work.'

I believe that when given a choice,

play is what children do,

always.

End of story!

In short, it isn't play if we are in charge.

We've devalued play to the point of collapse, just as we have severely impacted our planet's biodiversity—a play crisis playing out alongside a climate crisis.

Children's lives and schedules are becoming increasingly jam packed. From extracurricular and enrichment activities to numerous transitions between and through environments each day, there's not much space left for uninterrupted, self-directed play! Add a dose of devices to the mix, and some children are starving.

Starving for freedom, autonomy, starving for the opportunity to explore and play.

To understand how play is playing out in your kids' lives, it may be helpful to do a play audit. I have found that through this process, it is often found that play could be prioritised more. I have found that I am more able to advocate for and create space for play when I take notice of the opportunities I've created in the flow of our day for play.

On a typical day, how much can your kids freely play? Remember, we are talking free of adult agenda play, so a quick play in and around having brekky and getting ready to be out the door doesn't count.

How long after waking does your child have to wait before they can play?

How long is the longest stretch of uninterrupted agenda-free play on any given day? Interruptions include but are not limited to meals, bathing and self-care rituals, transitions to different care environments, chores, devices.

How often is unstructured, uninterrupted play factored into the outing when you leave your home?

How long do your kids typically play without seeking external stimulus?

You don't need to get too rigid with your audit. There's no requirement to create spreadsheets and pie charts to visually see where and how your children's days are structured.

What we want to do here is commit to curiosity.

Depending on the ages of your kids, you might find they are finding it difficult to play alone or with others without constant input, whether that be from you or devices.

If this is the case, it's important to note...

Our capacity to play is developed through the act of play.

The uninterrupted kind. This is an opportunity to stretch your child's play bandwidth gently. A great way to encourage more extended periods of uninterrupted undirected play is to get out in nature.

Have you ever noticed how time can melt away and the kids are extra engaged and creative when out in nature? Do you remember the freedom found in nature when you were small? It was where I felt most calm, and it still is. If I'm overwhelmed, get me by the sea, under a tall tree or where I can hear birdsongs. Nature's playground puts everything into perspective and unlocks our primal and intuitive selves through our senses.

Another consideration when pondering play is to notice when and where you are entering the play and annihilating it. It isn't play anymore when we bring in an adult agenda. Hands up if you've ever entered play and almost immediately started testing the child.

What colour is the ball?

Can you see a bird?

Guilty as charged...

No, it's not play anymore if you bring in the adult agenda. It's not play anymore if you start testing my knowledge. It's play annihilation.

So, what is a parent to do?

Slow down.

Slow down and remember what it's like to play.

Observe your kids. Through careful observation you'll get a front row seat to who your kids are in this moment.

If we big people can quiet our minds and mouths, much will be revealed.

When our kids play, they are 'learning.' A natural symphony of growth through osmosis and evolution. It may look like nothing to you, but for your child, it's purposeful. It may look like nothing, and that belief is what we've been sold. Do you remember how you saw play before you were told it was childish?

Yes, play, playing, and playfulness are incredibly important in childhood. The evidence is clear, but it's more than that. It's also a heap of fun. You don't need research to confirm that. You've been a kid. You've played from sun up to sun down. Do you remember?

Unbridled joy and frivolity are largely lost on the big people but relished by the small. Why do we reject our playful nature and become disconnected from play as we enter adulthood?

Is it because of the value and emphasis placed on work? If play is childish and work is mature, then perhaps this is how we come to reject our playful nature...

What's with the obsession in calling purposeful things 'work.'

Doing personal development, you are 'doing the work.'

Contributing to your society in a paid role, you are 'working.'

Mothering young children 'a mother's work is never done.'

What if we looked at how this unconscious messaging raised 'work' above all else? Imagine the human-beings we can raise if we shift our language and shift the emphasis away from 'work.' Would we raise a generation of kids who maintain the connection to their playful natures?

Let's journey back to your youth before you were programmed to see work as purposeful and play as childish, or a waste of time. When you were a kid, where was your place, the place you sought out to play?

How far from your home was it?

What were the distinguishing features?

Who was around?

What did you do?

For me, anywhere I could go on my bike was my place. My bike was freedom!

If I was having a hard day, I'd go for a ride.

When I felt disconnected and resentful, I'd go for a ride.

On days when I felt called to be alone, I'd go fast and far on my bike.

I couldn't tell you how often I ran away from home as a kid. I'd pack my bag, disappear on my bike full of fire in my belly and ride until my body found regulation. As I became calm and more regulated, I'd realise my plan was flawed and that I hadn't thought through complete self-reliance. I'd head for home to quietly unpack my backpack. Heavy work is a great nervous system regulation strategy. Look to your child with curiosity for clues as to what soothes their nervous system most effectively.

As the oldest child, I had plenty of opportunities to be with others, to be with and lead the play. Sometimes though, I wanted solitude, and my bike, plus the trees I could find and climb were my place to be. Who was with me depended upon my emotional state and what I was seeking in the moment?

Sometimes I would be with my brothers and the kids in the street, other times alone. One thing was for sure, there were no adults. Not because I didn't enjoy the company of adults, not because I was intentionally trying to stay away from them. But because play is just different with adults around. You know?

Were there adults in your place as a child? Or were the kids in charge? Leading and overcoming challenges that presented the best you knew how?

Undisturbed, uninterrupted, unhurried and undirected play is on the critically endangered list in our modern western world. Look around. Almost all the spaces children encounter, even those designed for them like playgrounds, are environments designed by adults. An adult interpretation of what children like - and need, don't forget that bit. Adults like to sprinkle in a bit of what kids need.

Children move through various environments throughout the day, and rarely are these spaces conducive to undisturbed, uninterrupted, and unhurried play.

How has play, and the opportunities children have to play, changed in your lifetime?

Can your children play similarly to how you did as a kid each day?

And most importantly, how can we advocate for our children to have daily opportunities for undisturbed, uninterrupted, unhurried play?

In our family, play is a core value. As a result, it gets a lot of airtime. I see the world and the various environments children find themselves in through this lens. Every day, it saddens me when I see how we, the big people, are letting our kids down when we fail to advocate for their right to play.

Undisturbed, uninterrupted, unhurried, and undirected play allows children to explore concepts, make meaning, and understand the world around them. It's also where they hone natural movement patterns, they need no instruction from us on how to move their bodies optimally. Children naturally seek out opportunities to walk, run, balance, jump, crawl, climb, hang and swim. There's no need for us to augment their play in order to offer them opportunities to do these things. Without instruction children naturally develop these locomotive skills alongside manipulative skills like lifting, carrying, throwing and catching.

What our kids need from us is access to environments that allow for free movement and repetitive opportunities to hone natural movement patterns. Over time, with repetition, skill and strength increase, but only if we provide movement friendly environments and live movement seeking lifestyles.

This leads me to ask, are there places where people in your home can hang and balance daily? Are your kids seeing you engaging in natural movement patterns? Do you walk barefoot and support your children to do the same? Do you run and jump and climb when the environment around you invites such movement? Do you actively bring the hanging and climbing opportunities into your home environment? As a species we are becoming increasingly sedentary, it's not only our bodies that are becoming stagnant, the impacts on mind, body and soul are vast. It's our environments that need augmenting, not our kids.

Natural movement patterns and play is what our kids need more of not more formal 'learning.' School readiness is garbage. It's unnecessary. Just as Zimmer frame readiness is garbage, so too is school readiness. No one needs to learn how to use a Zimmer frame before their mobility signals the need for a mobility aid.

So why do we see kids as needing to dedicate a whole bunch of energy and resources to get ready for the next thing? School readiness is just one of the ways we prime kids to always be getting ready for the next thing. We need to stop asking kids what they want to be when they grow up. In doing so, we will begin to unravel the future focus placed on childhood.

Childhood and who children are, as they are, is much more important than any adult driven or created 'readiness' practice. The antidote to too much too fast is play.

SECTION THREE

WHO YOUR KIDS
NEED YOU TO BE

CHAPTER ELEVEN

PRESENT

Presence, what an interesting and somewhat elusive concept for our modern world. It has been my experience that my capacity to cultivate present moment connection to myself has a direct influence on how present I am with others, especially my children.

In a world obsessed with being busy, what even is presence?

And what does presence or its absence look like in practice?

Here's the thing, your capacity for presence is invisible to the world, yet it's everything when gifted to someone.

When we feel seen, heard, and honoured, we are in the company of someone who is truly present in this moment, this experience, this energetic connection and exchange.

Earlier in this book we explored attunement. Here we take it deeper. Presence in parenting is a precursor to Attunement. Without presence, we are unable to attune to our kids. Imagine this scene. It's mid-morning, and everyone in the house is frustrated. You find yourself irritated and running some stories. You tell yourself things like.

"No one sees me."

"It's always like this!"

"I never get to do the things I need to do and no one even cares."

You are feeling resentful. The kids are underfoot, and you just can't get anything done. It's only mid morning, and you've decided the day is a write-off. It's a disaster.

Yep, I feel you,

I've been there too.

This is an example of family life in the absence of presence. No one is fulfilled. No one feels seen, heard or honoured. Put simply. There's no flow, and in the absence of flow, presence is unlikely.

Before you tear strips off me, hear me out. You may be thinking. "How can you possibly say I'm not present? My kids are with me, ALWAYS! How much more present do you want me to be? Honestly?"

I hear you. I feel you, and I am you. I am here to share with you that being with your kids doesn't automatically translate to presence.

Ever escaped into your phone and scrolled?

Ever hid in the bathroom for a few minutes of peace?

Ever felt completely tapped out and touched out?

Ever found an incessant and insatiable need to clean out those cupboards right this minute?

Yeah, me too, I get it. Parenting is tough.

I'm here to tell you that often we are with our kids without being present. Let me introduce you to an idea. Being available is not the same as being present. We mix the two up, viewing our availability to our kids as presence. Only it's not the same. You know the scenario well. The 157 interruptions while you hang out a load of washing result in a five minute task taking 30. It's feeling irritated by the level of noise and silliness while simultaneously missing the pure delight of the day's play.

You might find that you are 'with' your children a lot on any given day while not fully present in their experience. After all, there are plenty of other tasks that need to be done.

I find it helpful to recognise when I am in the same space as my kids but not deeply present. I do my best to remain available to my children when this is the case.

And most importantly, I make a mental note, a reminder that although I am with my kids, I'm not really 'with' them.

I am not present. Not really.

As parents, we can find ourselves in a perpetual cycle of availability, and it's tiring, taxing, and downright exhausting to be 'on' always... The constantly open loop of assessing and reassessing situations and dynamics to support our children in navigating the world. You find yourself constantly stopping what you are doing to help demonstrate a task or assist with that tricky puzzle. Availability is like parallel play for adults, and I am a sucker for getting sucked in. Invested enough in what the kids are doing to fool myself into believing I am being present, only I'm not.

As I write this, I am sitting in the passenger seat of our car while my husband drives the 90 minutes to town. I've got noise-cancelling headphones on, and the kids are set up in the back with all the options. They are content and engaged, yet I am still finding it difficult to switch off my availability.

My husband is chatting to our kids, and all of their needs are being met, yet I still find myself being pulled into their world. I believe we can sometimes confuse this 'always on' state for 'presence.' As mothers having one ear to our kids is very common. We are usually only one step away from dropping whatever we are doing.

This is availability,

not presence.

When we are present we are WITH them in every way. There's real value in getting curious about what presence instead of occupying space looks like in your home — the balance matters.

What does presence vs availability look like when you are tapped out, touched out, drained, exhausted, and overwhelmed? What then?

In these moments, it's been my experience that it's more about the quality of the questions and less about answers. We've been sold a lie about answers. We've been conditioned to believe that success = no unanswered questions. It's garbage. There's real value in sitting with the open loop of unanswered questions. Remember, this isn't school, no one is grading you. This is your life, and you can choose how you experience it. So ask away! Here's some of the questions I ask myself often.

Where am I? Like really? Am I here, where my feet are or am I elsewhere?

How will the energy of the home shift if I move into my kids with presence?

How will our experience of family change as a result?

What am I making it mean when I prioritise doing all the things instead of truly being with my children? Chaos or rigidity...

What stories am I telling myself about my worth?

Am I drawing a straight line between my output and my worth?

Does a tidy home = worth?

What do my kids need? Do I even know?

For me, presence goes well until it doesn't. I'm there, I'm all in and then like a switch, I'm not, and I'm floundering. Left wondering where 'it' went and how I can get it back. I find it's more about going forward with the capacity to see, hear and feel my kids instead of getting 'back' the thing. Instead of focussing on where 'it' went (presence) I allow myself to sit in the discomfort of an unanswered question alongside my commitment to be an imperfect human.

To be here, not in what has occurred and not in what is yet to come next is harder than it may seem. The what has been and what is yet to come are the thieves of presence, the pirates, you might say. They steal your presence, take it far away and bury it in some unknown place. Only to hand you a map filled with cryptic clues as to where to locate your treasure, the treasure that is your capacity for presence.

If you feel like you've also confused availability for presence or wonder where the pirates buried your treasure trove of present moment connection, you are not alone. It's a common thread in the conversations I have with Mothers.

I want to share a presence practice with you that has helped me a great deal. I like to call it "be here." When I am getting edgy or easily frustrated, I take this as the feedback that I need to stop for a moment to see what my kids are actually doing, not what I am telling myself they are doing. In these moments I remind myself to just be here.

Be here,
in this moment,
with what is!

Be here - What are my kids communicating to me in this moment?

Be here - What role am I playing in the situation?

Be here - What is the energy of the home?

Be here - What shifts when I become still?

The answers to these questions help me understand the present moment situation, which enables me to make my next move. Often nothing further is required of me. By being still and being here my children feel seen, heard, and honoured. Their present moment need is met by me simply becoming still and witnessing them.

It really is that simple. I'm reminded of the simplicity of this practice as I edit this very page. I've written and edited a lot of this book from the passenger seat of our car. On the day that I am here, editing this section, our son Wahri is teething and craving a lot of closeness. The distance between his car seat and me is almost enough to overwhelm his nervous system. He's holding it together, provided I am present and engaging with him. My capacity to edit is relatively non-existent, and I've needed to close my laptop and return to presence, return to the questions above and live my truth as shared here with you on these pages. It won't always be like this. For now, my full focussed, and deeply attuned presence is required. I need to be here. It is that simple, yet equally as exhausting and challenging!

Let's look at another example. You likely know this one well. Your toddler is hanging around your feet, trying to gain your attention. They are trying everything. You finally look down from what you are doing in exasperation and are met with a smile.

Your small person has been trying with all their might to bring you to the present moment, to bring your awareness and presence to them so they can communicate a present moment need with you. You sit down on the floor, and your child flops into your arms.

You connect. You see what they have been trying to show you. You meet their present moment need. Kids are experts at sensing when we are not with them. This is why you find it impossible to make a phone call without interruption or go to the bathroom alone. Our kids are hooked into our nervous systems, and they feel the disconnect when our presence is withdrawn.

Yet all 'presence' is not created equally. There's a spectrum. The spectrum spans from barely there through to deeply connected presence.

Everything melts away when you are deeply present and connected. You lose track of time, and you likely don't know where your phone is. There are usually no photos unless someone else is tuned into the moment's energy. It's that kind of energy. When witnessed, you can't help but capture it.

In contrast, the barely there end of the spectrum sees you unable to get a felt sense for your child. You have little to no awareness of how they feel or what they are doing. You are more focussed on how what they are doing frustrates you. You can't come far enough out of your own experience to feel them in these moments.

We often snap at our children from this place. We bark orders or project out onto them in unconscious ways. Cue mum guilt.......

I recognise that maintaining presence with our kids is difficult. I get it! I fall short often too.

We live in a world that champions being busy,

burnt out,

disconnected.

Parenting consciously is at odds with the way our society is geared. Parenting in this way is not the norm, nor is it easy, but it is worthwhile.

Our presence matters,

the way we show up matters,

and our capacity to reflect upon how presence shapes and influences our lives matters.

While pondering my relationships with presence I recall a day of profoundly connected presence. Naturally, I pulled it apart to understand it. Our son Wahri was eight months old. He and I were embarking on a full day of travel. 2 hours in the car, followed by a four hour flight and another two hours in a car at the other end.

Upon boarding the plane, everyone with young children was grouped down the back of the plane to avoid being too disruptive to the other big people. Within two rows of us, there were four other children under the age of two. Four other children who were to be confined to the laps of their adult travelling companions. We were fortunate enough to have a spare seat next to us on this flight. I was thankful that our freedom loving small person would have the space to move and feel independent.

Throughout the flight, I met Wahri with my full presence. With nothing more than my lap, a spare seat, and a few small objects to keep him content, I sat in full presence and deep attunement with him. We played and laughed and chatted with people around us. We were both enjoying ourselves, but mid-way through our flight, I could feel my energy and capacity for the intensity begin to wane.

I began to drift into my thoughts about this book and upon hearing a child scream was jolted back into the present moment. I looked around to see who it was, I knew by the cry that it wasn't Wahri. It was the small person one row in front of us. She was beginning to 'fuss.'

Her vocalisation and movements were beginning to become frustrated. She was about to crack. I looked to her parents with curiosity, had they clued on? Both Mum and Dad had headphones on, and although they were with their daughter, I could see they weren't with her. You know?

I know this because I too have been with my kids without being with them. I know this because I too, have finally clued onto what my child is trying to communicate too late. I, too, have faced a public meltdown that I could have avoided if I had been more present. I know this because I was present in this moment with what was around me, and I was able to see it unfold.

I share this story not to shame, blame or place any ill feelings towards these parents. I share it to demonstrate how the trajectory and the outcome of a situation like this depend largely upon where we sit on the spectrum of presence at any given moment. The question is, do we know when we are barely there vs deeply connected?

Our kids are hooked into our nervous systems. If we aren't present, it's almost impossible for our children to maintain regulation.

"She is so clingy."

"He's having a tantrum."

"She's always so needy."

"He lashes out."

When I hear these phrases and so many others, it's a clue and an opportunity to get curious about the presence of the big people. Ouch! When you find yourself thinking or saying these things ask yourself

Where was my focus?

What was I doing? Be specific.

What was happening in the lead up?

How equipped to be deeply present did I feel in that moment?

If through this process of introspection, you find that you were in the barely there state of presence extend kindness to yourself. Your capacity to recognise when you are barely there and the way your presence or lack thereof plays out in family life is life changing.

When we understand that we are co-creating the experiences of our lives with our kids we come to know that we can alter the course. Presence is interesting and often invisible. I encourage you to get curious about how presence plays out in your parenting practice and to get curious about how situations change when your presence shifts.

CHAPTER TWELVE

TRUTHFUL AND TRUSTWORTHY

For most of us, trust has been gained, lost, and muddled up more than we care to remember. If you, like me, feel that you can live your truth with reciprocal trust and respect, you have something valuable indeed. Coming to trust oneself, I have found, requires much unlearning. Let's look at your childhood to understand how trust, truth, being truthful and trustworthy play out in your parenting.

We've already explored how when you were a child, you collected values and beliefs and called them 'truth.' It wasn't your idea, most of those truths were gifted to you by others. The people who raised you had the most significant influence upon what you came to believe was true.

Likely, the people who raised you did so based on their upbringing, with the values and beliefs that were gifted to them on their journey to adulthood. Sounds idyllic, doesn't it? In actual fact what you've got there is a soup of lies, deceit and truth all mixed up. Is it any wonder our relationship with trust can seem a little off?

When you were a child who were the truthful adults?

Whose word did you trust? And why?

What did gaining trust look like for you as a kid?

What were the expectations in your house around telling the truth?

Did you believe it better to ask for forgiveness than ask for permission?

I ponder trust and truth often. I've pondered it a lot across my life, more so since I have been in a position of power as an adult. What I say, what I do, and the ways I show up in the world directly impact the small people who come into my sphere.

I take that truth very seriously. It sees me having conversations with children many would shy away from and sees my husband and I making decisions that rub up against the mainstream narrative. We believe the following.

To be truthful and trustworthy adults in the lives of our kids, we must be truthful and trustworthy from the start.

If we are to have teenagers who confide in us, we must be truthful and trustworthy from the start.

Living by our highest values and beliefs requires us to be clear about what we will and won't say to our children, from the start.

And this is where it gets tricky. When is a lie not a lie? What is harmless and what is not? Santa Clause, the Easter Bunny, and the Tooth Fairy, are these simply harmless white lies or is it a little more sinister? There is no right or wrong answer here, only your answer. For us, truth is truth.

A fat man in a suit delivering socioeconomically tiered pricing gifts to every child in the world with his chariot pulled by reindeer is not a lie we are willing to tell.

Yet while writing this book we found ourselves approaching the end of 2021 with little more clue about how we would do Christmas than the years before. You see our oldest, Hailey, is indoctrinated into Santa and all the others. While I was writing this book she carted a special magical box to Darwin for the school holidays 'just in case' her first tooth fell out. She tells us that it's the only way the tooth fairy will find her to swap the tooth for cash.

I don't know about you, but I find it incredibly difficult to see how this apparently magical being, that no one seems to have a visual representation of, can be amazingly magical AND equally useless at finding children who have lost teeth. But perhaps it's just me...

One thing is for sure, we won't indoctrinate Wahri, and so we dance. We dance with the space between being 'in' and 'out.' Before long, Hailey will find out the truth. She will know that we have lied. We will have to own that. We will be honest with her when that day comes. We will tell her we had a part to play in her belief about the fat man in the suit. We will explain to her how we came to understand that trust and truth are more important for us than a story handed down because 'it's just what you do.'

We will explain how we believed it would bring more hurt than good to come clean while she was three or four, and we will ask for her forgiveness. Hailey is growing up in two homes, homes she knows have different values and beliefs. She will likely be hurt by the incongruence between what we say and what we have done, truth and trust are core values in our family home.

So, what does our dance with the fat man and the rest look like in daily life? We are deliberately vague. We spin questions back to Hailey to gain her understanding or knowledge. We focus on presence over presents and speak of ritual and celebration instead of the fat man in the suit. You won't hear the classics around here.

"Be good or else..."

"Santa is watching."

"If you are good, Santa will..."

You will see us exchange homemade gifts made with love. We ask that gifts be labelled by the person gifting them, and we do the same.

My husband and I were raised with the Santa story. We hold no ill feelings for being raised in this way. We simply choose to live a different truth and let me tell you, it's not a truth for the faint of heart. If you come for the fat man, people will judge, project, and protect their truth with a single vision focus you've rarely seen.

We are quite used to witnessing the single vision focus of protecting one's truth in this house, and I suspect you may be too. After all, if you've picked up this book, I'll hazard a guess that you are the kind of person who cares not for the opinions of others about your values, beliefs, and subsequent choices.

I'm not saying you need to kill off Santa. I share our story and experience as just that, one family's story and experience with the trust and truth dance. What you do is up to you. There's no judgement here. Stand firm in your truth. That is my wish for you.

The fat man aside, the dance with trust and truth is intricate. How far you delve into the depths of the common deceptions perpetrated upon children is up to you. As the saying goes, it cannot be unseen once it's been seen. Know this, as you begin to see the world through the lens of pure truth in your relationships with children, you'll be forever changed.

It has been my experience that parents do not set out to deceive their kids. Often the parents I speak to are seeking to instil a value around trust, truth, and truthfulness in their kids.

Yet we lie.

We big people often lie to children, all while holding them to a higher standard of truth.

Why? If it's not willful deception, then why is this so?

Why do we profess to hold trust and truth in high regard while lying to kids?

To understand the depths of deception, let's look at some of the common lies told to children. You may or may not have had a part to play in these.

"Eat all your veggies, and you'll get strong muscles."

"If you tell lies, your nose will grow."

"This is the best drawing I have ever seen."

"The lights are on, that means the ride is out of order." – This one is told while walking past the pay per rides in the shopping centre.

"Be good, or Santa won't come. He's always watching you know!"

"I've got eyes in the back of my head."

"Babies come out of the Mummy's belly button."

"It's spicy." – we say while eating something sweet.

Often, I find that the lies told to kids fall into one of two categories.

Coercion and compliance or adult convenience.

We want our kids to eat the healthy food we provide. We know it is good for them. Coercion and compliance.

Lies perpetrated under the banner of coercion and compliance remain deeply entrenched. These lies are often carried forth from generation to generation with little or no conscious thought.

We want our kids to tell us the truth. It's frustrating and even infuriating when they don't. I've got eyes in the back of my head. Adult convenience.

If said enough in a compelling manner, the small people might just believe it. If they believe we've eyes in the back of our heads, they might modify their decisions and actions before we even have to catch them in a lie or doing the thing we have forbidden them to do. Make sense?

Lies on the adult convenience side are often a result of our fast-paced and overwhelming lifestyles. Or, because they are the kind of conversations that big people avoided when we were small, so we've no idea how to broach them. Take the belly button lie as an example. Speaking with children about conception, pregnancy, and birth isn't exactly a conversation of choice for most people.

Yet when our children come to us with questions, what they seek from us is the truth. They ask us to see them as worthy of and deserving of a truthful answer.

Imagine a moment if you asked a trusted mentor a question and received a nonsensical response intended to either garner your compliance or cleverly crafted for their convenience.

Would you feel valued?

Would you feel respected?

Would you trust them?

It's unlikely.

Of all the stories we adults tell ourselves, the lies perpetrated upon kids is the story I see people cling to the most.

It has been my experience that adult humans do not enjoy having the very foundation of how they engage with children shaken to the core.

But it's the very thing that has kids pulling away from adults. Do you remember? I do. When I cast my eye back to my youth, I remember recoiling when I saw, heard, or suspected an adult was lying to me. It eroded the very foundation of the relationship. Now I don't know about you, but this is not how I want my kids to feel in my presence.

But how do we shift it? I mean, lies are everywhere. You might even find evidence of coercive compliance or adult convenience in your core language. What then?

To stop lying we must first recognise the lies we tell ourselves, and our kids. So get curious, notice the little white lies reserved for adults, and look for alternative ways of being.

Got a toddler who loves to jump on the pay per ride train at the shopping centre? Yeah, me too. Weave a few extra minutes into the flow of the outing. Instead of distracting them or rushing past throwing an offhand comment about it being broken, gift your child the opportunity to explore and have a few minutes on their timeframe, running to their agenda. After all, it's unlikely that they have chosen that we are all off to the supermarket today.

Look for how you can create a win: win and maintain truth and trust in the family home. It's a fascinating experiment. In our house, we've come to a point where we look to the world for the lies told to kids. We pick them up in the language of adults around us and bring them home to unpack together. We do this to help orient us towards ever-increasing levels of congruence and truth. There's no judgement or looking down upon others. It's our way of eliminating lies that we haven't even considered yet. We get to explore the lies told to tweens and teens before our kids are that age. How brilliant. Its research and it's incredibly fascinating.

Another shift you can make to balance the scales on truth and trust with children is to apologise. To own your humanness and shortcomings.

Yelled at your child? Apologise.

Failed to follow through on something? Apologise.

Acted in ways you'd rather not? Apologise.

Lied? Apologise

Regardless of the transgression, apologise.

It's simple yet challenging. Do it anyway. Own your humanness. In doing so, you'll set your kids free. You'll pass on a blueprint to them that will serve them throughout their lives. And when you do apologise, you might be surprised to see that most kids are shocked to hear an adult apologise. It's simply not something children encounter often.

This is a truth I find all too sad.

Being a trustworthy adult isn't easy. It's a perilous journey that will test you no end. I recall my first big invitation to stand true to my values and go beyond the widely accepted narrative to be the trustworthy adult for a child who was hurting. It was early in my career as an Early Childhood Educator. To everyone else this child, let's call her Katie, was a problem.

Her 'behaviour' deemed unacceptable. Her capacity when compared to neurotypically developing children facing little to no adversity simply didn't hit the mark. I saw a child who was hurting, a child who felt all alone and a child who held a poor self-image. Being 'bad' was her truth, and it was consistently reflected back to her, therefore cementing it as truth.

A new year began. Katie and I were to spend the year together, alongside the other children of her age, you know, the one where four fingers are eagerly flung up. Upon receiving a handover from an Educator who had spent the previous year with Katie, I was presented with a folder that contained Katie's 'Behaviour guidance' plans. It was huge, it was full, and it was, in my opinion, entirely irrelevant.

My intuition told me this child needed connection, not correction. I knew if we were to truly support her, we would need to approach things differently. My first hurdle was getting families on board with my plan. People seek certainty that something will be successful, and I couldn't provide anyone with certainty. When Katie flipped her lid, families wanted assurance (certainty) that their child would not be hurt. Families wanted to know exactly how we would manage each situation and ensure that everyone was kept happy.

It was as if placing rigid rules and 10 step plans would be the answer, and that's what everyone around me wanted. If we could create enough structure to manage it, it would go away, right? But this was a child, a wildly complex and beautifully chaotic child who was doing her very best. It's only that her 'best' missed the mark as defined by society. Looking back now, I can see the brilliance, how I was forever changed through the experience of being the adult upon whom she could rely.

Yes, getting families on board was a challenge. Transparency and a truthful and trustworthy approach got us there. I was clear about what we were trying to achieve.

Connection.

As a team, we spoke at length, with families and with the children about what I called, at the time, 'family values.'

Children have already been conditioned to identify and categorise opposites at age four.

Good – Bad.

Up – Down.

Yes – No.

In – Out.

And at age four, if it doesn't fit with your narrative, which of course will be the good one, it must be bad, right? Subtle differences between family homes are one of the ways this plays out. Let's take dinner as an example. In some homes, a high value on connection may see meals eaten together, device and TV free, at the table.

However, in another family home, children may eat dinner and then after bedtime, the adults eat, or it may be dinner on the couch, dinner picked up on the way home. Now we all dip in and out of many different versions of dinnertime ritual, and it's unrealistic for us to maintain consistency each day. However, children will be able to identify the most consistent ritual. Asking kids how they see the seemingly mundane and unremarkable parts of daily life is a fascinating conversation, let me tell you.

Exploring the nuance of family values alongside the children was normalising differences and bringing awareness to different ways people do things. We discussed and agreed on our family values when we were all together. We asked ourselves questions and came up with answers that felt good for us.

How would we eat our meals?

How would we speak to each other?

What would be the boundaries?

And when we made mistakes, which we knew we would, how would we repair ruptures?

Within weeks, we began to see results for Katie and the entire group of children. We scaffolded, supported, and created space and safety to explore and test new ways of being together. Regardless of the situation or the day's trajectory, we maintained clear open communication, and above all else, we told the truth. If someone, big or small, was struggling with regulation, we made it visible. We spoke about our emotions and the way emotions influence decisions and actions. We made it safe to feel how you feel and showed up for the kids to co-regulate and support them in regaining equilibrium. I knew it was essential for us to focus on our language, the specific words we chose, and we supported children in developing the vocabulary to express how they felt.

You see, words like naughty, mean and bad do little to help a situation. But naming emotions and creating separateness between yourself and the emotion has an entirely different felt sense. We are not our emotions. Emotions come and go. They visit us. Sometimes we, the big people, can find it difficult to remember that we aren't our emotions. How do we expect our kids to know that emotions come and go if we forget sometimes?

Day by day, week by week, we saw calm contentment, children engaged and approaching others with empathy. This was my first big invitation to stand tall for a child and show up in ways that were a little outside the widely accepted narrative. This experience showed me exactly what is possible when we place trust in children and hold ourselves to a higher standard of truthfulness.

Trust and truth, it's worth pausing to ponder.

CHAPTER THIRTEEN

ACTIVISTS

What does being an activist mean to you? Depending upon your worldview and how you were raised, you may see tin foil hat wearing conspiracy theorist hippies in your mind. Activism is the act of using vigorous campaigning to bring about change, whether that be political or social. Put simply, you speak up. Kids need activists, people who will be vigorous in showing up and speaking up for them.

Activism for child rights issues requires us to set aside differences to benefit future generations. There's little I couldn't do in the name of child activism.

Child activism looks like advocating for a child's right to be seen, heard, valued, and respected. This pursuit fuels me, drives me forward, and has me questioning everything as I navigate the experiences of my life.

When I look back upon the story of my life, I see how I was gifted with many of my life's experiences to propel me towards being a child activist. I identify as an adult charged with the immense honour of being a voice for children.

Through this book, I hope that you come to see yourself as a child activist, firstly in your home and then more broadly in your community. To be the adult upon whom children can rely.

A great revolution is in motion, and our kids are the revolution, now more than ever.

Until the world hears them, let us listen to them.

Until they speak their truth, let us speak up for their rights.

Until they take the lead, let us amplify child rights injustices and inequality, subsequently solidifying our respect for them.

In short, let's be the voice for them until they can speak for themselves. Speaking up for children starts in the home, in the parenting decisions you make, the language you use, and in the environment you cultivate.

We know that kids are primed to absorb information. The situations, interactions experiences of their lives grow them. Growth through osmosis, remember. Mirror neurons start the process, children bathed in our powerful presence from birth. Everything we do, say, prioritise and place emphasis on is communicating to our children. Everything is an opportunity for growth to a child.

In our home, we strive to be attuned and responsive. We recognise that we are in constant communication with our children and that our capacity to be with our kids sets the tone. Our ability to be with our kids also has a lot of influence when we need to set boundaries and limits. When we fail to be attuned and responsive, when we fail to be with our kids, the wheels fall off. And it's these wheels I've seen fall off all too often in the relationship of family. Even the most conscious parent may fall into the trap of rigid instruction in chaotic moments.

You likely know rigid instruction all too well. It's likely the blueprint from your upbringing. It's the "because I said so" or "If you do that, then I'll do this" kind of compliance. You know, the behaviourist way of raising kids widely accepted as normal.

But what if there is another way? Another way that creates harmony and unity as opposed to separateness and misery?

What if, instead of instruction, we shifted our focus to motivation? Motivation has an entirely different energy, an entirely different intent, and often an entirely different outcome.

Let's take you, for example. If I were to motivate you to do something, I would first need to understand you. Understand your values, understand your beliefs, and understand how your brain works. Once I understood you and how your brain works, I would be well placed to speak to you in your values. Therefore I can motivate you to do something.

Instruction is different. It does not require me to know or understand you. In my opinion, the "because I said so" or "That's just the rules" approach to instructing children and requiring absolute compliance is something we ought to be wary of.

When we motivate a child, we support them with skill acquisition aligned with their values. When we instruct a child, we are telling them to be compliant. Compliance does not think. It waits for the next instruction.

Instructional learning is deeply entrenched in our society and our systems. For many of us this is what we invest a lot of energy and resources into unlearning.

I am watching my stepdaughter Hailey walk willingly into the abyss of instructional learning and conditioning the mainstream school system dishes out. Scoring her 'work' has become important as she navigates school. She recently asked me to go through the writing, drawing and games in her notebook to mark them from A+, which I am told is really good, through to F, which is an unquestionable failure with a capital F.

When I asked her if she was pleased with her efforts, she said, "of course, but I want you to mark it. To know if I got it right!" I did my best to get out of such as task, but it became apparent that my non-compliance would amount to a feeling of rejection. I reluctantly took up the red pen and turned to the first page.

How had we gotten here? I thought to myself. How, at age six, is my beautifully creative small person more interested in my opinion than how she feels about her efforts? Why is the process of her work being marked so important for her right now?

Over the next few minutes, I asked carefully curated questions and invited her to explain the process sitting behind the product I was viewing. She took the notepad off me about two pages in and started to mark her work. I was clearly taking too long and asking too many questions.

She came to a page she was visibly not impressed by. I saw her shrink. She sighed and wrote a large F, circled it slowly and sat staring at the F. After a few moments, the Hailey I know so well re-entered the room. She tore it out, scrunched it up and said, "I didn't do that one to be marked!"

It took every fibre of my being to not squeal audibly in delight! Instead, I smiled. Hailey had found a way to shift the heaviness in her body. She had demonstrated a capacity to navigate the system while finding ways to exist within it that feel good.

For me, my children doing things to gain external validation is sickening. I want their decisions and actions to be based on intrinsic motivation, not

external validation. Pause and ponder that one awhile...
What does child activism look like through the lens of
intrinsic motivation?

If we are to act as child activists, we must recognise
intrinsic motivation as the way forward. We must also
remember that we are raising a generation of children
who will need to overcome significant obstacles and
challenges if they are to undo the transgressions of
those who have come before them.

We are raising a generation of children who will encounter
problems for which we haven't got a point of reference.
For this reason and many others, we are raising a
generation of kids who need to be raised differently. To
succeed, we've got to raise them in ways that leave their
creativity, curiosity, and tenacity untouched.

How do we do that?

Equal parts activism and autonomy.

A little less instruction, a little more freedom.

But what does this look like with our very young children?
We can't exactly throw everything to the wind and hand
over the reins to our two year olds. If we did, we might
find ourselves eating ice cream for every meal, having a
bath at 11 pm and going for a wander around the garden
afterwards. I'm not saying boundaries and expectations
are out. I am saying that we best beware of why we are
setting said boundaries and expectations. "Because I
said so" is no longer an adequate explanation.

The number one way we can be of service to children is to view the world through their eyes. Everything from seeing the wonder of the natural environment to recognising the ways our modern world and urban landscapes do our children an immense disservice. This is activism, right? Seeing the issues from their perspective and vigorously campaigning to bring about change.

Almost all the spaces young children occupy are geared towards ease and convenience for us, the adults. There are hardly any spaces designed for children BY children. Let's take playgrounds as an example, these are spaces 'for' children, right? But they are created by adults and are apparently convenient to families. However, rarely do these spaces truly hit the mark for children.

Swings are often positioned to place young children squarely in the kick zone. Poorly designed shade or a complete lack thereof renders slides unusable for large parts of the day. Fun fact, your skin peels off your bare butt in Darwin if you go down a hot slide. I know. It happened to me as a young child.

How about a failure to co-locate bathrooms in a way that facilitates an adult supervising the bathroom door and the playground simultaneously? These design deficits detract from the usability, safety, and 'convenience' of these spaces. We can overcome many of the barriers if only we would slow down enough to observe and see the spaces through the eyes of a child.

Swing kick zone a problem? Raise the swing area, creating a physical barrier that places them beyond the reach of our crawling infants.

Yes, parental supervision and support are essential, but poorly designed spaces lead to parents hovering over young children, doing these children a disservice. When we hover over young children, their capacity to feel capable and navigate the space diminishes. They come to rely on us to 'help' them conquer obstacles and challenges within their capacity to conquer alone. Hello learnt helplessness. We created you.

Purposeful spaces for children, especially the very young, are spaces where children can explore without adults constantly saying,

no,

watch out,

be careful.

And the list goes on. Spaces where adults are not constantly on guard for the purposes of risk minimisation. I'm not advocating for a risk-free world. My standpoint on risky play is quite the opposite. But there's a difference between a risk and a hazard. Our world is full of hazards for the very young, and the impact on their development is dire. Let's focus on hazard management and allow our kids the freedom and autonomy to understand risk.

Our son Wahri was born on 20 acres at Dundee Beach, an hour and a half from Darwin. We lived in a tiny house surrounded by the picturesque and rugged territory landscape.

From birth, Wahri had ample room to move.

To explore.

To test theories.

And he thrived and continues to thrive in environments that provide for his free movement and expression.

Living an hour and a half from town allowed us to revel in a peaceful secluded lifestyle. But you've got to go to town for supplies at some point. Town days were pretty straightforward from a free movement standpoint at first. All we needed was a soft rug to pop down wherever we were. As Wahri became mobile, we found ourselves with fewer free movement opportunities on town days. We needed to make solid plans around the flow of our day to advocate for and provide for Wahri's right to free movement.

We found that he was spending most of the day contained on town days. He was restricted and placed into containers for the convenience of adults and the way our society is set up. It was challenging to find other options. His day was being spent held in arms, strapped into a carrier or car seats. Not developmentally optimal nor ideal for his temperament and personality.

How could the comforts of town be so detrimental to his development? We began to seek out spaces that allowed Wahri the opportunity to move unhindered during our long town days.

Car seat, ok, that one is necessary. Subsequently, how long is he spending in his car seat? A minimum of 3 hours, not including the running around for errands and gathering resources like the groceries. Ok, before we've even left the block, we've got 3 – 4 hours contained. Next up is shops. We've got to go to several places. Where can he get on the ground? For how long? And what time of the day will we be at these locations? Playgrounds aren't always a viable option in Darwin unless you want to overheat your kid.

I began to structure our day around putting Wahri at his best advantage for unrestricted movement, and although this increased his opportunities to move, I was still falling dismally short. Public spaces are not designed to put the very young at their best advantage. Not everyone will find themselves in the position we found ourselves. Not everyone will have their child out and about in public spaces for 8 – 12 hours for a 'town day', but the impact of poorly designed spaces is, in my opinion, a universal one.

We have a society of families raising very young children who are making decisions based on the way our spaces are, not on what is ultimately best for children.

Going to the shops? Best put the pram in the car. It won't be appropriate for my child to be on the ground.

Going to the supermarket? We can't have the toddler walking around. They'll grab everything off the shelves.

Lunch with a friend? Where on Earth can we go where my child can play freely?

Going on a flight. How on Earth will I get through airport security on my own with an infant and a laptop that will need to come out of its bag? And all this after you've walked from one end of the airport terminal to the other to drop off your car seat at the inconveniently located oversize baggage counter.

Having a haircut and colour? Salons are not kid-friendly. I'll have to have someone else care for my child.

Attending a conference, function or event? Best leave the kids at home.

These are child rights issues, and human rights issues. If you look, you'll find them everywhere. Our children are growing up with constant messaging that they should be seen and not heard, that they need to be quiet and calm and act like tiny adults when out in public. Only our kids aren't tiny adults, they are kids, and we are setting them up to fail. How many variations of these have you heard?

'Those kids are out of control!"

"That mother needs to control her kids."

"This is not a place for children to play."

So, what can we do about this human rights issue?

What if, instead of projecting the problem out onto children, we looked at spaces through their eyes. Asking ourselves questions like.

Is there a safe space for very small children here?

Does this environment cater for children?

Can children play here?

Will children feel like they belong here?

Can children be themselves here?

I believe that if we saw the world through the eyes of a child, we would make different choices, the policy would shift, spaces would change, and we would see a reverence for childhood and a child's right to occupy all spaces. Can you see it?

But what can we do right now in our daily parenting practice you may ask. We can bring awareness. Take notice of the decisions you make when you go out in public with your kids and ask yourself if these choices are for the benefit of children or the convenience of adults.

Here are some examples of how we do it in our home. We are being met with a variety of responses in the community. Above all else, we are bringing awareness to the issue at hand.

We occupy space unapologetically. When Wahri was nine months old, I delivered my 'Honouring Infancy' workshop at an Early Childhood Conference. Wahri has been with me, since conception, by choice and as aligned with our values. The conference was to be no different. We booked my husband a delegate ticket and attended as a family. When packing for the day, a blanket and basket of toys occupied space alongside my laptop. His needs met alongside mine.

We found a spacious position with easy access to the walkway during the keynote addresses in the ballroom. We laid out our blanket to sit, play and occupy space. As a result, Wahri adapted to the environment, and he played. Many people commented on how 'well' Wahri had done throughout the day. And it was true. He had navigated the largest crowd he had ever seen, explored spaces seemingly unremarkable to the adults, and captivated many with his presence.

But he had done this as a result of our intentional choices, choices centred around setting him up for success. We utilised the speaker preparation room when we observed the pace and noise level threatening to overwhelm him. We followed his lead as he explored and moved closer to him if something unexpected (to him) occurred.

He fed on his timeline, just like every other day of his life. This saw him on the boob as I began my 45 minute presentation mid-afternoon.

And it was fine.

It was more than fine,

it was natural, and it further enhanced my core message.

Through the example of occupying space and setting Wahri up for success in attendance at an 'adult' event, it opened the loop for several delegates. Before long, discussions of inequality of access for children and the impact of segregating children from daily societal activities were being had. We were hypothesising about what a truly inclusive world looks like.

The way I see it, this is an invisible human rights issue. Once you are big enough to understand human rights and marginalisation, you have lost the capacity to identify as a child. As a result, the invisible problem continues.

I believe we can bring the invisible into sharp focus through child rights activism, and it starts in the home.

Child activism asks us to occupy space,

to challenge the narrative largely accepted.

Raising children IN society,

not excluded,

nor segregated.

To live a life that challenges the perception that it isn't appropriate for children to be active and integral society participants.

This is activism, and our children deserve it.

What will you do?

I invite you to seek ways to put your children at their best advantage through your choices. Our children bathe within our daily actions, the big and the small. Make decisions that support your child's success, not the choices socially acceptable by some pre-determined and largely archaic definition of 'right.'

Breastfeed in public if you feel comfortable. It's your child's right to be nourished. What other people think is their issue, not your concern. I'm yet to have someone come up to me and express their offence at witnessing me eating a meal. Why is it any different for a child being nourished at the breast?

Take your children with you everywhere that you are comfortable doing so. Occupy space by putting down a rug and a few books or toys. Your children have the right to BE in society, in public areas, and be seen for who they are in all their unique glory. You are a child activist. You get to decide how that looks for you.

CALL TO ACTION

Our son Wahri's birth was the catalyst for the creation of this book. Throughout the first year of his life, I was called upon to create this introspective guide for you. In doing so Wahri has called me into my true purpose and asked me to stand tall as a child activist. We've been gifted the opportunity to change the narrative, to reparent ourselves as we raise our kids.

I believe that to heal the planet is to raise children who will create a world unrecognisable to us.

The question is, are you willing to be an adult upon whom the children of the world can rely? Can you sit in the space of the unknown, the unanswered and unchartered? Are you willing to step back in order for children to step forward?? Are you courageous enough to upset adults in pursuit of that which is of critical importance for children?

I am, and if you've made it through to here, I believe you are too. Let's raise our babies in ways that both feel good and lay the foundations for what will be a world unrecognisable to us.

I'd love to connect with you and come to understand your story. I believe there is great power in sharing our stories. To connect with me simply scan this QR code to go to my website. From there you'll be able to connect with me or link through to my socials.

ACKNOWLEDGEMENTS

Throughout my life, I have been fortunate to have the opportunity to explore and expand upon my understanding of children and childhood.

I'd like to acknowledge and thank some of the great minds, whose wisdom, research, and life explorations I've drawn upon in cultivating my life and in writing this introspective guide for you. Coming to understand the concepts explored, uncovered, and lived experiences of these people has fundamentally changed the way I do life, through osmosis. Never underestimate your impact.

To Dr Daniel Siegel you made brain research make sense to me. If I'd been told 25 years ago that the pocket guide to interpersonal neurobiology would become my favorite choose your own adventure book I'd have laughed. Your contribution to humanity is vast.

To Dr John Demartini you've shown me that what I once viewed as being weird or strange is my unique genius and in doing so I've been able to unlock my true potential. Thank you.

To Carlie Maree, I adore you. Your humility and deep care for humanity in all its forms fuels the child activist in me to keep going. You've shown me how to take things a little less seriously and that has assisted me to get out of my own way. You help people to see beyond the confines of their mind to the land of plenty, thank you.

And finally, to my husband Brendan. I am in awe of you. You've shown me what it is to be loved and held unconditionally, as I am, free from judgement. This book would not have been possible without your unwavering belief in me. I've received many gifts from you my love and by far the greatest is bearing witness to you as a father. I love you, thank you xx

Some of the greatest minds of our time have dedicated their lives to uncovering and unmasking the unknown parts of childhood and for each of them I am grateful. It is through the dedication of those mentioned and many more that we can come to be well equipped to raise children who thrive, if it wasn't clear within the pages of this book allow me to make it abundantly clear now. The way we raise children must change if we are to continue as a species.

Thank you!

Zoe Haack – Child Activist.

CPSIA information can be obtained
at www.ICGtesting.com
Printed in the USA
BVHW030343020722
641195BV00011B/1025

9 780645 480900